TAIWAN
in Pictures

Alison Behnke

Twenty-First Century Books

Contents

Lerner Publishing Group, Inc. realizes that current information and statistics quickly become out of date. To extend the usefulness of the Visual Geography Series, we developed www.vgsbooks.com, a website offering links to up-to-date information, as well as in-depth material, on a wide variety of subjects. All of the websites listed on www.vgsbooks.com have been carefully selected by researchers at Lerner Publishing Group, Inc. However, Lerner Publishing Group, Inc. is not responsible for the accuracy or suitability of the material on any website other than www.lernerbooks.com. It is recommended that students using the Internet be supervised by a parent or teacher. Links on www.vgsbooks.com will be regularly reviewed and updated as needed.

Website address: www.lernerbooks.com

Twenty-First Century Books
A division of Lerner Publishing Group, Inc.
241 First Avenue North
Minneapolis, MN 55401 U.S.A.

web enhanced @ www.vgsbooks.com

CULTURAL LIFE 44

► Religion. Holidays and Festivals. Literature. Visual Arts. Music, Theater, and Movies. Food. The Sporting Life.

THE ECONOMY 56

► Services and Trade. Industry. Agriculture. Forestry and Fishing. Transportation and Energy. Media and Communications. The Future.

FOR MORE INFORMATION

Library of Congress Cataloging-in-Publication Data

Behnke, Alison.
    Taiwan in pictures / by Alison Behnke.
        p.   cm. — (Visual geography series)
    Includes bibliographical references and index.
    ISBN 978-0-8225-7148-3 (lib. bdg. : alk. paper)
    1. Taiwan—Pictorial works—Juvenile literature. I. Title.
DS799.13.B44 2008
915.124'9—dc22   2006101990

Manufactured in the United States of America
1 2 3 4 5 6 - PA - 13 12 11 10 09 08

INTRODUCTION

The small, mountainous island of Taiwan lies off the southeastern coast of Asia. Although it is not large in area, it has developed into a sizeable economic power. It is one of the world's top producers of computer technology, and its industries create and export manufactured goods to markets around the globe. But Taiwan was not always an international force. In fact, throughout its history, outside powers have often controlled it. In the seventeenth century, Taiwan—which Europeans called Ilha Formosa, or "beautiful island"—shifted between Chinese and Dutch control. Two centuries later, a war between China and Japan brought Taiwan into the Japanese Empire in 1895. The Chinese regained administrative authority over the island in 1945.

But this beautiful island would not remain under full Chinese control for long. Clashes erupted on the Chinese mainland between two opposing forces—the Chinese Communists and the Nationalist troops of the anti-Communist Republic of China (ROC).

(Communism is a political and economic model based on the idea of common, rather than private, property.) By 1949 the Communists were threatening the Republic of China's security on the mainland. The ROC's leadership—headed by a military officer named Chiang Kai-shek—withdrew to Taiwan. There, they were beyond the reach of the Communist forces who had taken over much of China. They hoped to regroup and mount a new challenge to the Communists. Chiang formed a government-in-exile for the ROC on Taiwan. Also in 1949, the Communists established the People's Republic of China (PRC) on mainland Asia.

The arrival of the NationBab el-Mandebalist leaders and thousands of their followers added to the mixture of people on Taiwan. The largest ethnic group among modern Taiwan's 22.8 million people are—like the Nationalists—of Chinese ancestry. They came to the island over the course of several centuries, before the 1900s. The Nationalist Chinese who arrived in 1949 and afterward comprise the

CHINA

Matsu
Islands

East China
Sea

Keelung
River

Keelung

Taipei
Taoyuan   Yangmingshan   Badouzi

Hsinchu

Hsintien
River

Lower
Tanshui
River

Gueishan
Island

Suao

Taiwan Strait

Kinmen Island

Taichung

Sun Moon
Lake

Penghu
Islands

Choshui R.

Taiwan

Makung

Peikang

Penghu Channel

Pitan

Coral
Lake

Tsengwen
River

Fort Zeelandia   Tainan

Maolin National
Scenic Area

South China
Sea

Kaohsiung

Tungkang

PACIFIC
OCEAN

Kenting
National
Park

Luzon Strait

Inset map

Legend

Taiwan

⊛ Capital city
• City

0   40 Miles
0   40 KM

N

second-largest portion of the population. The smallest group is made of people who are sometimes called aborigines (original inhabitants). These residents are descendants of the island's earliest peoples.

As the second half of the twentieth century began, the governments of the ROC and the PRC agreed that Taiwan was a province of China. They also agreed that China should be reunified under a single government. The two regimes disagreed, however, about whether that government should be Communist or Nationalist. At first, most members of the United Nations (UN) supported the Nationalist government in its claim to authority over China. In the 1970s, however, more and more nations in the UN began recognizing the Communist PRC. The UN expelled Taiwan from its members, and fewer countries kept up diplomatic ties with the ROC.

Despite these setbacks, Taiwan maintained an impressive level of economic growth. By the late 1980s, the Taiwanese enjoyed one of the highest standards of living in Asia. In addition, the island's government used its commercial power to stay involved in international affairs. Even when it was diplomatically isolated, Taiwan continued doing business with many nations.

The status of the island's relationship with the People's Republic of China remains unresolved in the 2000s, however. For this small but beautiful island, this big issue will probably continue to dominate politics for years to come.

THE LAND

The total territory of Taiwan covers 13,969 square miles (36,180 square kilometers). This area makes the ROC approximately the same size as the U.S. states of Massachusetts, Rhode Island, and Connecticut combined. Taiwan's main and largest island is, itself, called Taiwan. The ROC's government also controls dozens of smaller islands. They include Kinmen (sometimes called Quemoy), Matsu, and the Penhgus (formerly the Pescadores).

The island of Taiwan is about 240 miles (386 km) in length, with a width ranging from 60 to 90 miles (97 to 145 km). To the west, the waters of the 100-mile-wide (161 km) Taiwan Strait separate the island from the southeastern coast of mainland China. The East China Sea washes against Taiwan's northern coast. Across these waters to the northwest are the Ryukyu Islands belonging to Japan. The Pacific Ocean forms Taiwan's eastern boundary. To the south, the South China Sea lies between Taiwan and the Philippines. No town or city on Taiwan is more than 50 miles (80 km) from a major body of water.

Topography

Taiwan's main island is made up of three distinct regions: the mountainous center, the western plain, and the eastern coastal strip. The craggy mountainous center dominates Taiwan's landscape. Mountain ranges cover about two-thirds of the island. The largest is the north-south Chungyang Shan, also known as the Central Mountain Range. It runs down the middle of Taiwan for the island's entire length. Peaks in east central Taiwan rise to heights of more than 12,000 feet (3,658 meters) above sea level, sometimes dropping sharply toward the ocean. Ranges in the southwest are lower, topping out at about 8,700 feet (2,652 m). The island's highest point is the south central peak of Yu Shan. Also called Jade Mountain, it has an elevation of 13,113 feet (3,997 m).

Taiwan's western plain is home to most of the island's people. The flat, fertile region lies between the Taiwan Strait and the rolling foothills of the mountains. This low western region is narrow in the

CHINA

East China
Sea

Matsu
Islands

Lower
Tanshui River

Keelung
River

Hsintien
River

Gueishan
Island

Kinmen Island

Taiwan
Strait

WESTERN PLAIN

Taroko
Gorge

CHUNGYANG SHAN

EASTERN COASTAL STRIP

Sun
Moon
Lake

Choshui River

Penghu
Islands

Penghu Channel

Taiwan

Yu Shan

Coral
Lake

TAITUNG RIFT VALLEY

South China
Sea

Tsengwen
River

PACIFIC
OCEAN

CHINA
INDIA VIETNAM
JAPAN
Ryukyu Islands
TAIWAN
PHILIPPINES
PACIFIC
OCEAN

INDIAN
OCEAN

AUSTRALIA

0   1000 Miles
0   1000 KM

Taiwan

Feet	Meters	
9843	3000	Mountains
6582	2000	Uplands
3281	1000	
1640	500	Lowlands

Elevation

N

▲ Mountain peak

0   40 Miles
0   40 KM

Luzon Strait

north and widens as it extends southward. Large deposits of alluvium—a mixture of sand, clay, silt, and gravel—make the western plain a highly productive farming region.

Taiwan's eastern coastal strip is made up of two parallel sections. An inner region known as the Taitung Rift Valley hugs the edge of the Chungyang Shan. The rift valley lies along a crack—or rift—in the earth's surface that runs from northeast to southwest. Streams running from the nearby mountains cross this valley, which rarely exceeds 10 miles (16 km) in width.

The outer section of the eastern coastal strip is also about 10 miles (16 km) wide. Facing the Pacific Ocean, it consists of rolling hills made up of sandstone and limestone. Taiwan's eastern shore has few natural harbors. As a result, the island has few ports.

Nearby Islands

The Penghu Islands are located in the Taiwan Strait, approximately 30 miles (48 km) off of Taiwan's southwestern coast. Since 1949 the Nationalist government has administered the Penghus. More than sixty islands exist in all, but only about twenty of them are inhabited. The island named simply Penghu is the largest. Combined, the Penghus cover an area of about 50 square miles (129 sq. km). Volcanic activity formed the islands, but underwater erosion before they emerged from the sea left them with a flat topography. They lack rivers as well as significant natural resources. About 100,000 people live on the Penghus altogether, with most of them on the main island.

Cacti grow on **Penghu Island.**

The shallow waters that surround the Penghus are ideal for fishing. In addition, warm temperatures in this region of the Pacific Ocean favor the growth of natural coral. Coral reefs surround the islands. These reefs form good harbors and strong barriers against the huge waves created by typhoons (Pacific hurricanes).

Located on the main island, Makung is the largest urban center on the Penghus. Oceangoing ferries and small airlines connect Makung with cities on the island of Taiwan. In addition, several bridges link the bigger islands to one another.

Both Kinmen and Matsu are island groups that lie near the coast of southern China's Fujian province. Inhabitants of rock-strewn Kinmen raise livestock and grow sorghum (a cereal grain), peanuts, and sweet potatoes. Matsu, on the other hand, is not suitable for farming. Fishing is its main industry.

Rivers and Lakes

Most of Taiwan's rivers begin in the Central Mountain Range and flow westward. Because fewer than 60 miles (97 km) of territory lie between the mountains and the coast, these rivers' courses are short, steep, and swift. Sometimes they run through dramatic gorges on their way to the sea. Large commercial ships cannot navigate Taiwan's waterways. However, dams harness the energy of many rivers' rushing water to produce hydroelectric power. The island's rivers also help irrigate farmland.

The longest waterway in Taiwan is the 105-mile-long (169-km) Choshui River. The Choshui waters the fields of central Taiwan. The Lower Tanshui River flows for about 100 miles (161 km) south, toward the city of Tungkang. The Tsengwen River runs westward to the Penghu Channel. It travels some extremely steep sections along its 85-mile-long (137-km) course. Other rivers include the Hsintien and the Keelung.

Taiwan has few natural lakes. Located in the foothills of the Central Mountains, Sun Moon Lake is the largest freshwater lake on the island. It is also the site of one of Taiwan's first hydroelectric plants. Coral Lake lies in southwestern Taiwan and is fed by the Tsengwen River. Its name comes from its many-fingered shape, which resembles a piece of coral.

A PRECIOUS PLACE

Sun Moon Lake is not only Taiwan's largest lake but also one of its most important cultural sites. The lake and the land around it are the traditional homeland of the Thao people—the smallest group of ethnic aborigines remaining in Taiwan. In the Thao language, the lake's name is Zintun. Lalu Island, which lies in the center of the lake, is a sacred area for the Thao.

◎ Climate

High temperatures, uncomfortable humidity, plentiful rainfall, and strong winds are the main features of Taiwanese weather. In general, the climate is subtropical in northern and central Taiwan and tropical in the south. Summers last from about April to September and are humid. The average summertime temperature is approximately 80° F (27° C). Winters (October to March) are usually mild, with temperatures only dropping to about 60° F (16° C).

Rainfall is abundant in Taiwan. More than 100 inches (254 centimeters) water the island in an average year. The eastern coast receives more rain than the western coast. Small areas in the extreme north and south also get large amounts of precipitation. The island's central mountains sometimes receive snow.

Taiwan's rains arrive as a result of monsoons. These moisture-bearing winds blow across the island in two seasons. Winter brings the northeast monsoon, which in some years can carry as much as 50 inches (127 cm) of precipitation per month to the northern half of the island. The southwest monsoon arrives in the summer, bringing up to 40 inches (102 cm) of rain per month to southern Taiwan. Monsoon rains fall at a steady rate in the north, while the south often experiences periodic, torrential downpours.

Taiwan also lies in the path of typhoons. The typhoon season lasts from May to October. The strong winds of these storms often destroy settlements as well as crops. However, most of the typhoons blowing from the South China Sea do not hit the island directly.

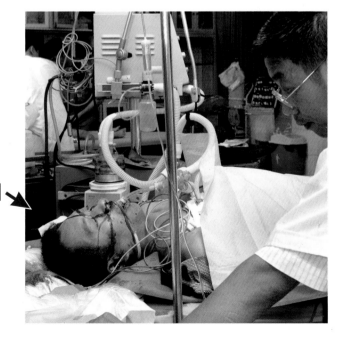

In August 2004, **Typhoon Aere** dumped 4.5 feet (1.4 m) of rain on some parts of Taiwan. Hillsides crumbled in its two-day storm. A doctor leans over a man who was injured when the typhoon damaged the construction site where he was working.

Another threat to Taiwan is earthquake activity. Because the island is situated along a crack in the earth's crust, about 1,500 earthquake tremors occur during an average year. Taiwan has only one active volcano, which forms the very small island of Gueishan. Gueishan Island is located just off of Taiwan's northeastern coast.

⊙ Flora and Fauna

Forests cover more than half of Taiwan. Dense vegetation blankets most of the island's mountains. Pine, spruce, hemlock, and cypress trees cover many elevated areas. On the lower regions of the mountains, stands of oak, teak, acacia, ebony, camphor, and sandalwood trees thrive. Scattered amid the dark green foliage of the hardwoods are many clumps of bamboo, which is actually a species of tall grass. The foothills are thick with tree-sized ferns. Lilies, azaleas, and orchids also brighten these low slopes.

A Taiwanese woman harvests calla lilies in Yangmingshan, Taiwan. The high altitude is perfect for growing the lilies, and about two million bloom annually.

The mountains of Taiwan shelter wild boars, black bears, apes, and monkeys such as the Formosan macaque. The Formosan serow is a small wild goat that also makes its home in Taiwan's mountains. Panthers prowl some of the island's forests. The relatively sparsely populated eastern coast provides habitat for wildcats and several species of deer. Various birds, such as kingfishers and larks, fly Taiwan's skies. Marine life in Taiwan's waters includes coral, whales, sea turtles, and many tropical fish.

One of the most unusual animals to call Taiwan home is the pangolin— a scale-covered, ant-eating mammal. These shy creatures are armed with tough front claws, which they use to rip open the earthen mounds of ants and termites. They have no teeth, but instead use their long tongues to collect and eat their insect prey. When threatened, pangolins curl up into a ball to present only their hard, sharp scales to the attacker.

Natural Resources and Environmental Challenges

Taiwan has few natural resources. The island's forests, however, make up a valuable asset. The rich farmland of the western plain is also an important natural resource, as are the fish-abundant ocean waters around the island.

But it often seems as though Taiwan's environmental challenges outweigh its resources. The island's industries and its many cars— especially in the population-dense north—make air and water pollution a serious problem. Pollution also contributes to a rising number of endangered animals in Taiwan. Heavy logging causes habitat destruction. Hunting is another threat, but posters on some parts of the island do warn hunters that laws protect certain wildlife species, including pheasants. The flying fox—a large fruit bat—is also protected but may already be extinct in Taiwan.

Cities

More than 75 percent of Taiwan's 22.8 million people live in cities. The largest of these urban areas is the capital, Taipei. This city boasts a population of about 2.6 million. Located at the intersection of the Hsintien, Keelung, and Lower Tanshui rivers in northern Taiwan, Taipei is the island's administrative and industrial hub.

Immigrants arriving from China's southern province of Fujian founded Taipei in the early 1700s. The city's industrial development began in 1885, when Taipei replaced Tainan as the island's capital. In addition, Taipei experienced considerable growth under Japanese rule (1895–1945). In modern times, the city's factories produce electrical equipment, textiles, plastic, steel, chemicals, machine tools, and rubber products. Taipei is also an important stop on the island's west coast railroad and has both an international and a local airport.

Taipei is home to many cultural sights. One well-known local landmark is the National Palace Museum. Thousands of Asian artworks brought from China in the late 1940s fill this museum's galleries and halls. In addition, the Fine Arts Museum is known for its extensive collection of oil paintings, sculptures, and other artworks.

With a population of 1.5 million, Kaohsiung is Taiwan's second largest city. Chinese settlers from the provinces of Fujian and Guangdong originally formed Kaohsiung in the fifteenth century. The city eventually came under Dutch control, and later Japanese rule. With an excellent natural harbor, Kaohsiung has become Taiwan's leading port. This south-

TALL ORDER

Taiwan's capital city has boasted an especially dramatic skyline since 2004, when the Taipei 101 skyscraper (right) opened. There are several ways to determine what is the world's tallest building, depending on whether the measurement reaches the top floor, rooftop, or tip of the spire or antenna. By any measure, however, the Taipei 101 is among the top three tallest structures on the globe. Named for its 101 stories and designed by architect C.Y. Lee, the apartment building stands nearly 1,474 feet (449 m) from the ground to the rooftop. The spire on its top adds almost 197 more feet (60 m) to the structure's total height.

Learn more about urban and rural Taiwan, its flora, its fauna, its climate, and more. Go to www.vgsbooks.com for links.

ern city boasts modern dock facilities and is home to the island's largest fish market. A rail and highway endpoint, Kaohsiung is also an important industrial center that contains steelworks, ironworks, shipyards, and oil refineries.

In the 1700s, Chinese immigrants settled a section of west central Taiwan, where in modern times the city of Taichung is located. It ranks as the island's third largest urban center at just over 1 million people. Taichung grew in importance when a harbor was built 10 miles (16 km) from the city in the 1970s. Expressways connect Taichung to its port facilities. Factories in central Taiwan transport most of their goods through the city's shipping outlet on the Taiwan Strait.

Taiwan's southwestern city of Tainan is home to more than 755,000 people, making it the island's fourth largest city. Founded by Dutch explorers in 1624, it is also an important historic site. Tainan was the capital of the island until 1885, when the government moved to Taipei. Its many traditional and religious buildings include a temple in honor of Confucius, the founder of one of Taiwan's main faiths. Tainan remains a major cultural center of the island.

The Confucius Temple in Tainan, Taiwan, was completed in 1666. Parts of the temple have been rebuilt to repair damage from earthquakes and wars.

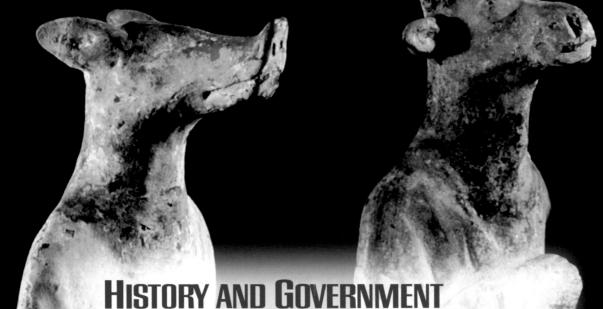

HISTORY AND GOVERNMENT

Much of Taiwan's history cannot be separated from that of China. The fortunes of the two areas were intertwined for centuries, and events on the mainland influenced many of the island's changes over the decades. This influence continues in present times. Yet Taiwan also has its own unique character, historical events, and traditions.

Archaeological finds, including stone tools and pottery, suggest that Stone Age peoples inhabited Taiwan around 28,000 B.C. Some experts believe that these early groups originated on the Chinese mainland. Others speculate that peoples from the Malay Peninsula of Southeast Asia were Taiwan's first immigrants.

⊙ Early History

The first known Chinese written records of Taiwan seem to identify the area as Liuqiu. According to these records, a Chinese emperor in the Tang dynasty (family of rulers) sent expeditions to

Liuqiu in the early A.D. 600s. His troops found settlers who used the slash-and-burn technique to clear land for farming. After cutting and burning vegetation, the island's farmers planted crops such as rice, millet (a cereal grain), and beans. A main leader and several subleaders shared authority in ruling the islanders.

Under the Song dynasty, which reigned from 960 to 1279, the Chinese continued to explore and settle Taiwan and the nearby Penghu Islands. Coins and pieces of pottery from the Song period have been found on the Penghus. These artifacts suggest that migration to the islands began in about the eleventh century. The abundance of fish in the waters surrounding the Penghus may have attracted Chinese fishing crews to the islands.

Several developments on the mainland led to increased exploration of the Penhgus and Taiwan in the thirteenth century. The Mongols—a nomadic group of skilled horse riders and archers from northern China—chased the Song rulers southward to Hangzhou, in present-day Zhejiang province. The Song government settled in an area near the South China Sea. From there, it encouraged better shipbuilding and greater seafaring activity. In addition, Chinese scientists invented the magnetic compass. This valuable tool allowed sailors to travel more confidently in the waters between China and Taiwan. All of these factors enhanced China's ability to navigate the seas.

Mongols and Mings

The Mongol conqueror Kublai Khan eventually defeated the Song rulers. He founded the Yuan dynasty in 1279, and its leaders sent expeditions to Taiwan in 1292 and 1297. Seafarers regularly visited Taiwan and traded with the islanders, but they did not settle there. During this period, a Chinese official governed a small but growing Chinese population on the Penghus, making the islands part of the Chinese Empire.

In 1368 the Ming dynasty succeeded the Mongols as mainland China's rulers. Meanwhile, migration to the Penghus continued in the fourteenth and fifteenth centuries. By the mid-sixteenth century, fishers and traders from China's Fujian province had discovered Taiwan's value as a fishing and commercial site. However, the Ming did not consider the island an official part of China.

Migration to Taiwan from Fujian increased in the late Ming period. In 1589 and 1593, the Ming government issued trading licenses allowing merchants to go to Taiwan. Unlicensed ships also crossed the strait to exchange the mainland's porcelain, cloth, and salt for Taiwanese deerskins and fish.

Japan also showed interest in trade with Taiwan in the late sixteenth and early seventeenth centuries. Japanese naval forces tried to occupy the island in 1609 and 1616. But, for a variety of political and economic reasons, the Japanese government soon chose to isolate their island nation. This decree ended Japan's contact with Taiwan for more than two centuries.

European Contact

During this period, European adventurers' exploration of Asia also increased. Portuguese navigators traveling southward from Japan to the Malay Peninsula sailed along Taiwan's coast. It was these Portuguese sailors who named the hilly land Ilha Formosa, meaning "beautiful island." For centuries thereafter, Europeans called the island Formosa.

Dutch merchants also became interested in Taiwan in the 1600s. They hoped to establish a new port near Chinese trade centers. By

The **Ming dynasty's navy** sails away to fight Japanese pirates in this drawing from that period.

1622 the Dutch East India Company (which oversaw business in Asia for Dutch investors) had set up a military base on the Penghu Islands. But the Chinese drove the Dutch out of the Penghus. The Dutch moved to southwestern Taiwan in 1624 and built Fort Zeelandia there a few years later. This fort became the foundation of a settlement near Tainan.

Meanwhile, Spanish settlers landed in northeastern Taiwan in 1626. The Spanish would eventually build two forts there. But within about fifteen years, Spain turned its attention to unrest in its other Asian colonies, including the Philippines. By 1642 the Dutch were the only Europeans on Taiwan.

The Dutch encouraged sugarcane planting. They also taught local workers to extract camphor (a chemical used in making medicines) from the island's many camphor trees.

PIRATES OF THE TAIWAN STRAIT

Pirates sailed the waters between China and Taiwan for centuries. In the 1500s, piracy around the region increased. Numerous merchants, including some from foreign nations, traveled the seas near Fujian province. Their heavily laden ships were attractive prizes to pirates operating from the Penghus and Taiwan. These pirates also raided the southeastern coast of the Chinese mainland. Some of them were Chinese themselves. Among Chinese pirates, Lin Daoqian and Lin Feng were the most famous. They plundered ships in the mid-sixteenth century, and both established outposts on Taiwan.

In addition, the Dutch made Taiwan a major center for trading Chinese goods with Europe and with other Asian nations. The Dutch East India Company built a trading station at Taoyuan in the northwest. At this site, locally produced deerskins, sugar, and rattan (palm stems) were sold to merchants from China and Japan. Europe received Chinese porcelain from Taiwan. In return, European nations and their colonies shipped pepper, linen, tin, and opium (an addictive drug) through Taiwan to China.

Seeking a larger labor force on Taiwan, the Dutch encouraged Chinese mainlanders to move to the island. They also introduced new crops and livestock and improved farming methods. Dutch missionaries (religious teachers) converted some islanders to Christianity, setting up schools to teach the local population more about the faith.

The Dutch substituted European-style organization for the islanders' traditional government and made workers labor under harsh tax laws. To subdue the islanders—as well as the Chinese—Dutch leaders often used physical force. Resentment flared on the island, and in 1652, about 15,000 people on Taiwan rebelled against the Dutch. Carrying little more than bamboo spears and small knives, the rebels were defeated within two weeks by the well-armed Dutch forces. Two-thirds of the rebels died.

Zheng Chenggong Arrives

Meanwhile, events in China affected the Dutch, as well as Taiwan. The Ming regime had become increasingly oppressive by the mid-seventeenth century. Ming rulers heavily taxed rural residents, and revolts protesting the taxes broke out in several areas of China. Taking advantage of the unrest, another group—the Manchu—overthrew the Ming. The Manchu set up the Qing dynasty in 1644.

In parts of southern China, Chinese who were loyal to the Ming leaders organized resistance movements. Among those who resisted Qing rule was Zheng Chenggong. Zheng fought against the Manchu and their Qing dynasty for twelve years—even after the Qing conquerors had put down all other resistance. He maintained an outpost on Kinmen and used this base to launch several attacks on the mainland.

Eventually, however, Zheng faced the reality of Qing control of the mainland. In 1661 he and a small group of followers fled to Taiwan. There they hoped to regroup and renew their war against the Manchu. Zheng's forces joined with Chinese islanders dissatisfied with Dutch rule. Together they seized Fort Zeelandia and expelled the Dutch from the island in 1662. But soon after removing the

Dutch, Zheng died. His son Zheng Jing succeeded him as ruler of Taiwan.

The younger Zheng's rule, which lasted until 1678, was harsh. He heavily taxed Chinese and native islanders alike, often beyond their ability to pay. Punishments for most crimes—even for cutting bamboo illegally—were severe. Islanders staged several uprisings during Zheng's reign, although Chinese immigrants did not join these revolts. After Zheng Jing's death in 1678, his son took over. But many islanders refused to accept his authority. This instability enabled the Manchu to claim Taiwan as Chinese territory in 1683.

The Qing Government

Although their Ming predecessors had shown little interest in Taiwan, the Qing dynasty valued the island's location and its agricultural potential. In addition, Taiwan already had thousands of Chinese residents. In 1684 Qing rulers officially made Taiwan part of Fujian province, and large-scale emigration from China began soon afterward.

Nearly all of the newcomers came to Taiwan from the farming areas of southern China. Qing officials who arrived to run the island, however, had more diverse backgrounds. In fact, sharp differences existed between average immigrants and the island's Qing leaders. The newly arrived farmers began to cultivate land almost immediately, bringing formerly untouched areas of Taiwan under the plow. Between 1684 and 1735, farmers cleared and planted a wide strip of land along the northwestern coast, as well as a large region in the south. These new farms claimed land from the islands' original inhabitants. The farmers pushed these indigenous peoples farther inland, away from the coastal areas.

Unlike average Chinese immigrants, Qing administrators had little interest in developing the island. These officials served no more than three years in Taiwan before returning to the mainland. They spent much of that time collecting money through illegal schemes. With widespread governmental corruption, the island became a place of lawlessness. Robbery and civil unrest were common.

Thus, although Taiwan became more commercially important by the nineteenth century, its people grew increasingly dissatisfied. Fifteen major rebellions occurred between the 1700s and the mid-1800s. Smaller uprisings took place even more frequently. This local mistrust of the Chinese government allowed foreign powers in the region to use Taiwan as a base for challenging the Qing dynasty. Both the British and French threatened to take over the Penghus and Taiwan in the mid-1800s. In response to these challenges, the Manchu chose to change the way they governed Taiwan.

Find out more about the ancient and modern history of Taiwan. Go to www.vgsbooks.com for links.

Reforms and Japanese Gains

In about 1880, the Manchu sent Liu Mingchuan to Taiwan to act as governor. Liu was a talented administrator. He sponsored the construction of the island's first railway, between Taipei and the nearby port of Keelung. Under Liu's direction, workers established a telegraph network, improved ports, and developed a postal system. The governor encouraged industry, mining, and foreign trade. These advances made the island more manageable, and in 1885 the Qing government made Taiwan a full-fledged province of China. That same year, they moved the island's capital from Tainan to Taipei.

During this period, Japan attempted to take over areas of Chinese territory. In 1894 this struggle for territory erupted into the Chinese-Japanese War. The better-trained and better-equipped Japanese army won an easy victory over the Chinese troops. In 1895 the Treaty of Shimonoseki ended the war. The document gave the Japanese control of Taiwan and the Penghus. A new Japanese governor and his officials arrived on Taiwan. While the Qing dynasty still ruled most of the Chinese mainland, the dynasty's 211-year reign over Taiwan had ended.

Under Japan

Japan's desire to control Taiwan was part of a larger plan to make Japan an important imperial power. Japan's leaders hoped their nation would soon rival empires in Europe, Russia, and Asia. But local opposition to Japan's possession of Taiwan was strong. Guerilla warfare, waged by small independent forces, targeted the Japanese. This opposition continued off and on for the next twenty years.

At first, Japan used the island mainly as a source of staple food crops, especially rice and sugar. Later the Japanese decided to develop Taiwan industrially. They built hydroelectric plants, railways, and paved roads on Taiwan. Japan also constructed textile mills, an oil refinery, paper factories, fertilizer plants, and other facilities.

The Japanese also made unpopular changes, however. For example, they strongly encouraged the Taiwanese to use the Japanese language and follow Japanese customs. Nevertheless, because of their many improvements, they gained the cooperation of many islanders.

◎ ▶ Events across the Strait

Meanwhile, changes were taking place on the mainland. The Chinese revolted against the Qing in 1911, forcing the Qing emperor to resign. This revolution signaled the birth of the Republic of China (ROC).

In southern China, the leaders of the revolt against the emperor set up a new government. The government's leader was temporary president Sun Yat-sen (also called Sun Zhongshan). Yuan Shikai and a group of warlords (military commanders) controlled the rest of China. They paid little attention to what was happening in the south.

Sun Yat-sen

Sun developed three principles for the Kuomintang (also spelled Guomindang), or Nationalist Party. These three principles were nationalism (strong loyalty to one's own nation above others), democracy, and common wellbeing. The Kuomintang opened local branches around China. These branches built regional support by recruiting urban workers and rural dwellers as members. The party also organized an army in Guangzhou (once named Canton) under a young officer named Chiang Kai-shek (also spelled Jiang Jieshi). Hoping to unite all of China, the Kuomintang worked together with the leaders of the

This photo of **Chinese president Yuan Shikai** *(center)* and his fellow officers was taken immediately after his inauguration on March 10, 1912.

Chinese Communist Party (CCP), which was established in 1921. The CCP was committed to Communist goals. These goals included government control of resources and equal distribution of resources among citizens.

Sun Yat-sen died in 1925, leaving the task of unification to Chiang Kai-shek. In 1927 Chiang brought the warlords under his authority. Soon afterward, he and the Nationalists broke relations with the CCP, which had tried to set up a rival government.

Having united China under a single government, Chiang next began modernizing the country. He ordered the construction of new roads, railways, and factories. But the Nationalist government offered little relief to rural workers who were deep in debt to their landlords. Furthermore, the Kuomintang did not allow urban laborers to set up trade unions. The CCP, on the other hand, promised to introduce both land reform and unionization. These pledges gave the Communists a popular advantage over the Nationalists.

Changes on Taiwan

In the 1930s, the Nationalists faced further setbacks. The Japanese seized China's mineral-rich northeastern provinces in 1931, followed by parts of the eastern coast in 1937. From 1937 to 1945, the nation struggled against the Japanese invasion.

These **Republic of China troops** fought Japanese troops for control of the Republic of China in the 1930s.

Meanwhile, relations between the Japanese and the Taiwanese worsened. The Japanese prohibited the use of Chinese dialects (language variations) and treated the island's inhabitants as second-class citizens. Many Taiwanese residents resented these threats to their way of life.

By the 1940s, Japan had made Taiwan into one of its military bases. At first, the Japanese used the island as a supply spot for their troops fighting against China. Later, the site was ideal for making quick aerial raids to bomb U.S. stations in the Philippines during World War II (1939–1945). Because of Taiwan's strategic importance, the Allied forces of the United States and Britain, who were fighting against Japan, bombed it heavily. The attacks demolished many Japanese-built factories and power plants, and destroyed airfields and roads.

Japanese control brought Japanese culture to Taiwan. The outside rulers taught the Japanese language in schools, introduced Japanese foods, and filled the cities with their own style of public buildings. Japanese religious shrines began to appear throughout the island.

Ultimately, Japan's military might proved to be too little against the Allied forces. Following the Allied use of two nuclear bombs against Japan, the nation surrendered to the Allies in 1945. Among its losses were its Asian colonies. Taiwan once again became a province of China. The Nationalist government appointed a new governor of Taiwan. But postwar conditions caused conflicts between islanders and the central government's officials. For example, the new arrivals took over the island's finest houses, as well as businesses that war had not destroyed. At the same time, prices soared, while food supplies plummeted. As Taiwan's average people grew hungrier and more dissatisfied, a major uprising broke out against the central government. Chiang responded in 1947 by arranging for food relief. He also replaced the governor with new and better leadership.

Conflicts on the Mainland

The Nationalist government in China had survived Japan's attacks, but it still faced conflicts with the CCP. Although the two groups had cooperated to defeat the Japanese, civil strife erupted after the war's end.

At first, Chiang was in a better military position than the CCP. However, his policies made him unpopular among the people. His troops seized land from farmers, and government officials grew rich by stealing foreign aid. Famine and floods also plagued the Taiwanese, further complicating Chiang's situation.

The CCP was then led by a young Communist revolutionary named Mao Zedong. Mao took advantage of Chiang's unpopularity to promote Communist ideals. These beliefs included shared landownership and the outlawing of privately owned businesses. Meanwhile, the party consolidated its forces in the north. Communist forces launched a strong offensive against Chiang's troops in 1949. With Communist troops advancing, Chiang realized that defeat was near. He ordered weapons, money, and industrial supplies to be moved to Taiwan. From the island, he intended to continue the fight against the CCP.

Mao Zedong

But the CCP won firm control of the mainland. In Beijing on October 1, 1949, Mao established the People's Republic of China (PRC). In December Chiang left for Taiwan, along with 800,000 soldiers and about 2 million civilian followers. From the beginning, this

In 1949 **defeated ROC soldiers retreat** from PRC forces.

group of exiles saw themselves as the only legitimate Chinese government. Their greatest goal was to recover the Chinese mainland.

Chiang's Taiwan

Chiang's arrival on Taiwan was the beginning of major changes on the island. Once considered little more than a remote part of China, Taiwan became the headquarters of the Nationalist government. But Chiang himself still saw Taiwan as a Chinese province. He did not support independence for the island. Indeed, both the PRC and the ROC agreed that Taiwan was part of China. They disagreed, however, about which government should run China. Nations around the world took sides on the issue. Some, such as the United States, supported the ROC's strong anti-Communist stance. Others, including the Soviet Union (a large Communist union including Russia), backed the PRC's claims.

Chiang enacted widespread land reform programs on Taiwan, based on the principles of Sun Yat-sen. New laws redistributed land among small landowners. Increased farm production soon followed. The government sought to create an agricultural economy that would provide raw materials and money for industrialization.

Hampering these efforts was friction between longtime Taiwanese and more recent Chinese arrivals. Many Taiwanese doubted that reunification with the Republic of China was in their best interests. Independence movements arose, but Chiang's troops harshly put them down. Eventually, it became illegal to promote the idea of an independent Taiwan. Chiang did ease tensions somewhat by appointing a few Taiwanese to government positions. Nevertheless, the Kuomintang kept a firm grip on the island and its people. Chiang soon instituted martial law, giving the military broad powers to control Taiwan's residents.

Chiang Kai-shek sits erect on his horse's back.

Bombs from the Communist People's Republic of China hit Kinmen Island, Taiwan. During the 1950s, the PRC also frequently attacked Taiwan's Matsu Island, which lies close to the shores of mainland China.

The Shifting Tide

Chiang's new state received a boost from large amounts of U.S. economic aid. These funds allowed Taiwan to begin repairing and expanding its industries. The United States also offered the ROC's leaders military protection against attack—which Taiwan feared from the PRC—by signing a mutual defense treaty in 1954.

This protection was not offered without reason. During the 1950s and 1960s, the Nationalist government and the PRC waged a war of might and propaganda (ideas spread to strengthen the control of one party or system). Tensions skyrocketed and resulted in brief military conflict during the First Taiwan Strait Crisis in 1954. A second crisis followed in 1958. Mao's PRC frequently shelled Kinmen and Matsu. Meanwhile, the ROC built up its forces for war against the PRC and made occasional raids on Fujian province. Additionally, the anti-Communist United States and the Communist PRC had recently been on opposite sides of the Korean War (1950–1953). The U.S. Navy patrolled the Taiwan Strait to prevent the PRC from taking Taiwan by force.

All the while, Chiang kept a firm grip on control. He was reelected president of the ROC in 1954, and again in 1960. (He would also be reelected in 1966 and 1972.) In fact, he did not permit any strong political opposition on Taiwan for several decades. The Kuomintang and a few pro-Nationalist parties were the only political organizations allowed to pursue public office. Resistance to the regime lessened, however, as Kuomintang policies spurred high economic growth and improved living conditions. By 1965 Taiwan's remarkable industrial progress allowed it to fund further economic expansion. By the 1970s, the people of Taiwan had one of the highest standards of living in Asia.

During these years, Taiwan continued to claim that the ROC was China's rightful government. Many nations, including the United States, supported this claim. In addition, the ROC was a member of the United Nations.

In 1970, however, the situation changed. After twenty years of negotiations, Canada established diplomatic relations with the PRC in hopes of improving Canadian trade. Meanwhile, Italy, Belgium, and other nations began recognizing the PRC as China's legitimate ruler. In 1971 the UN expelled Taiwan's representatives and seated PRC officials in their place. And the next year, Richard Nixon became the first U.S. president to visit Communist China.

These moves troubled Chiang. He increasingly withdrew from public view. He died in 1975, still insisting that China—including Taiwan—should be under a Nationalist government. Chiang's son Chiang Ching-kuo replaced him as Taiwan's leader. Then, in January

Taiwan's **premier Chiang Ching-kuo** *(right, lifting his hat)* visits soldiers in the ROC garrison on Kinman Island for Chinese New Year in 1975.

1979, the United States—long Taiwan's strongest ally—officially recognized the leaders of the PRC as China's legitimate rulers. The United States said that China should solve the question of Taiwan.

Different Directions

In 1980 the United States did not renew its security treaty with Taiwan. Soon after, the United States also reduced the quantity of weapons that it sold to Taiwan. These changes alarmed the Kuomintang, which believed that the island remained under constant Communist threat. Indeed, the PRC had not ruled out the use of force to unify Taiwan with mainland China. As a result, Taiwan built one of the largest defense systems in the world. All young men had to complete military service, while Taiwanese women could voluntarily join the armed forces. Although still heavily dependent on U.S. arms, Taiwan also began to produce its own weapons.

At the same time, Chiang Ching-kuo focused on economic development and political reforms rather than on retaking the mainland. He encouraged more native Taiwanese to participate in the government. He also allowed several opposition political parties to exist. They included the Democratic Progressive Party (DPP), which called for Taiwan to establish itself as an independent nation, completely separate from China. In 1987 Chiang took another major step by ending martial law on Taiwan.

Chiang Ching-kuo died in early 1988. He was succeeded by his vice president, Lee Teng-hui. Taiwan's economy continued to grow during

Lee Teng-hui is a native speaker of the Hakka language. Hakka is a local dialect of Chinese that is distinct from Mandarin Chinese, the official language of the island. Lee's 1988 rise to the presidency marked the first time that a Hakka politician headed the ROC government.

Lee's presidency, and the country also increased trade with the PRC. By 1989 Taiwan was trading $3.4 billion worth of goods with the PRC through Hong Kong. Hong Kong, a port on China's southeastern coast, was at that time not an official part of the PRC. In 1995 Taiwan traded directly with the mainland for the first time.

Despite this progress, friction between the ROC and the PRC remained. A Third Taiwan Strait Crisis erupted in 1995, when the PRC tested a series of missiles not far from Taiwan. Although the PRC's leaders stated that they would not attack the ROC, many Taiwanese saw the tests as a clear attempt to frighten them and their government. The United States agreed. U.S. leaders sent the aircraft carriers USS *Independence* and USS *Nimitz* to patrol the waters around Taiwan. At the PRC's stern warning, however, the ships did not enter the Taiwan Strait. The crisis had largely passed by summer 1996, but unease remained.

Also in 1996, Taiwan's citizens chose Lee as president in the ROC's first direct presidential election. (The government's National Assembly had appointed earlier presidents.) But charges of corruption plagued Lee's Kuomintang. The party lost support among the voters, maintaining only a slight majority in the legislature. Rival parties, including the DPP and the New Party gained strength. They threatened to break the Kuomintang's hold over the Taiwanese government.

At the **Tsoying Navy Base in Kaohsiung, during the Third Taiwan Strait Crisis,** soldiers and armored tanks line up in a show of strength on September 27, 1995.

⊘ Ongoing Tensions

Following the 1996 reelection of Lee Teng-hui, Taiwan's government further changed in 2000. Chen Shui-bian of the proindependence Democratic Progressive Party was elected president, bringing an end to more than half a century of Kuomintang dominance. He won the election by a small margin, however. Many members of the government and the population still supported the Kuomintang.

Chen's stance on Taiwan's relationship to China also led to internal friction. Because Taiwan already functioned largely as an independent state, Chen believed that it was unnecessary to formally declare independence from China. This position was unpopular with hard-line members of his own Democratic Progressive Party, who favored a clear declaration. It also displeased those who still favored reunification with China. Debate swirled around the issue in the early 2000s. Chen's controversial position nearly cost him a second term as president, when in 2004 he was reelected by a margin of only 0.2 percent. In addition, conflict over the independence issue flared between Taiwan and mainland China again in 2005. That

FIERY POLITICS

On March 19, 2004, Chen and his vice president, Annette Lu, were campaigning in Tainan for the upcoming election. As the pair waved to onlookers from an open jeep, a member of the crowd suddenly fired a gun at them. Chen was shot in the stomach, while Lu received a wound to her leg. Their injuries were not life-threatening. The very next day, Chen and Lu were reelected—but they won only by an extremely narrow margin.

Some anti-Chen observers found the whole incident suspicious. Some even suggested that the shooting had been staged to win Chen and Lu sympathy votes. While this theory remains unproven, Taiwanese voters continue to discuss it.

A **bullet hole** remained in the windshield in front of President Chen Shui-bian (*standing, second from left*) and Vice President Annette Lu (*standing, second from right*) from the assassination attempt on March 19, 2004.

year the PRC passed a law stating that it would use force against the ROC if Taiwan declared independence from China. The law met with outrage among Taiwanese. They made a statement of their own in early 2006 by eliminating the National Unification Council. This group had been in charge of overseeing eventual reunification.

For decades, the ROC's Nationalist government regarded itself as a government-in-exile that rightly ruled all of China. Many Taiwanese have begun to give up this claim, however. Most notably, President Chen Shui-bian publicly disagreed with this position.

Meanwhile, Chen's government faltered. His party lost regional and local elections around Taiwan. And a new challenge arose when corruption charges were made against Chen's wife and three officials. Chen was implicated, but as president he could not be tried. Although Chen has claimed innocence, observers expect him to be charged after leaving office. Protests erupted against him in autumn 2006, and the scandal dragged on in 2007.

Government

The Taiwanese Constitution was originally created in 1947, but it underwent several amendments during the early 1990s. Instead of being chosen by the former legislature, called the National Assembly, the president and vice-president win four-year terms in a direct popular election. In fact, by 2005 the National Assembly had been abolished and disbanded.

In the 2000s, President Chen Shui-bian called for further constitutional reform. He suggested that the document no longer represented the reality of modern Taiwan. While many Taiwanese supported the idea of a new constitution, both the PRC and the United States expressed unease with the plan. The constitutional debate continues.

Under the existing constitution, Taiwan's president is head of the armed forces, negotiates foreign treaties, and issues emergency orders when needed. The president has authority over the five branches of government, which are called the Five Yuans. The president nominates the premier, who is the head of the Executive Yuan, which is responsible for policy and administration. The Legislative Yuan acts as the main law-making body. Members of the Control Yuan oversee the government's efficiency, while the Examination Yuan functions as the civil service. The Judicial Yuan has supreme, high, and district courts.

In keeping with the view that Taiwan is a subunit of the ROC, the island also retains a provincial government. This system includes a governor and a provincial council. The duties of this government have gradually been reduced, however, and there have been calls to eliminate it.

THE PEOPLE

Taiwan is home to 22.8 million people. This number gives the small island a population density of 1,633 inhabitants per square mile (631 people per sq. km). Such a high density places Taiwan among the top ten densest nations in the world. In comparison, China has an average of 355 people per square mile (137 per sq. km), while Japan fits 876 people into each square mile (338 per sq. km). However, 78 percent of Taiwan's residents live in urban areas. In fact, more than 10 percent of all Taiwanese are in Taipei. As a result, the capital and other cities are even more crowded than the average population density suggests. The island's many mountainous areas, on the other hand, have a far less dense concentration of people.

Ethnic and Language Groups

About 98 percent of Taiwanese people are ethnically Chinese. Within this group, most are descendants of the Chinese who emigrated from the southern Chinese provinces of Fujian and Guangdong more than

three hundred years ago. Those with ancestors from Fujian make up the majority of ethnic Chinese on Taiwan. They speak a variation of the southern Chinese dialect Amoy. The immigrants from Guangdong, on the other hand, brought the Hakka language with them. Most Hakka speakers live in northeastern Taiwan. Distinctions between these two groups of Taiwanese lie mainly in their languages.

The next large wave of people to arrive on the island came in 1949 and the following years. These twentieth-century arrivals came from all parts of the Chinese mainland, but most spoke Mandarin Chinese. This dialect is used in large areas of China, including the region near Beijing. Chiang Kai-shek made Mandarin Chinese the official language on Taiwan. (Mandarin Chinese is also the official language of the PRC.) It has been taught in all schools on the island since the 1950s. By the 1980s, an entire generation of islanders spoke Mandarin.

All Chinese dialects use the same written form. In written Chinese, symbols called ideograms represent ideas instead of sounds. These symbols are arranged in vertical columns that are read from top to bottom, beginning with the right-hand column.

Nearly all of Taiwan's Chinese residents have a shared cultural identity. This identity includes similar religious ties and a common written language. However, Taiwan's original ethnic groups, who are descendants of the area's first inhabitants, have their own cultures. Together, these indigenous ethnic groups make up less than 2 percent of the island's total population.

Indigenous communities include the Ami, Paiwan, Atayal, Bunun, Saisiat, and Thao peoples. Most of them look different than islanders of Chinese ancestry, although ethnic mixing has occurred between indigenous and Chinese groups. Most ethnic communities are located in mountain villages, with the exception of the Ami, who live on the eastern coast. Traditionally, these native peoples farm and follow their own religious practices. They do not understand each other's languages, the roots of which experts place within the Malayo-Polynesian family. This language family also includes Malaysian and Filipino dialects.

> While Mandarin Chinese remains the official language of Taiwan, many residents speak local dialects in their homes. These language variations include Hakka and Min Nan. In addition, a small number of indigenous Taiwanese speak ancient aboriginal languages.

The leader of **Smangus, a remote Atayal village in Taiwan,** arranges food offerings on an altar. The offerings are for Mangus, the residents' common ancestor for whom their village is named.

Along **a busy street in Kaohsiung, Taiwan,** people mingle with cars and motorcycles.

▶ Daily Life

Taiwan's spectacular economic growth in the late 1950s and the 1960s increased many islanders' incomes. It also affected urban and rural lifestyles. Modern Taiwan is a highly industrial and technologically advanced society, and this sophistication is evident in islanders' daily lives.

In urban Taiwan, cars and motorcycles crowd city streets. While they are signs of prosperity, these modes of transportation also produce traffic jams and pollution. City populations also grew over the years. Modernized farming methods freed many young Taiwanese to move to urban areas to earn higher wages. Some rural Taiwanese families have members who live in the cities and visit the countryside on weekends. But those who live in rural villages also enjoy modern comforts and conveniences. Even remote farmhouses, for example, boast antennas to improve the reception of urban television broadcasts.

Other aspects of daily Taiwanese life are similar to those in other industrialized parts of the world. Clothing styles are similar to those in Europe and North America. Entertainment in the island's cities includes U.S. and Chinese films, as well as international and modern music. Taipei, in particular, boasts many Internet cafes. Customers at

A clerk serves a customer with tea to go at a modern **teashop in Taipei.**

PERFECT BALANCE

For many Taiwanese, an important aspect of daily life—from their homes to their workplaces and beyond—is feng shui. This art is the placement of objects in harmony with the environment and with *qi* (pronounced "chee")—the energy or life force of all things. Objects arranged according to feng shui's principles include buildings, pieces of furniture within a room, or items upon a desk. If these things are positioned incorrectly, it is believed that unhappiness, bad luck, and even tragedy may result. Correct balance, in contrast, can bring good fortune. While it has its origins in ancient China, feng shui is more popular in modern Taiwan than in the PRC.

these cafes can use computers and high-speed Internet connections as they sip tea or coffee.

Domestic dynamics in Taiwan also reflect modern values and lifestyles. Family ties—which were once built around moral and social obligations—have loosened. Members of an extended Taiwanese family may still live close to one another in urban apartment buildings. But the government is taking on more responsibility for the care of older people—a duty traditionally belonging to family members.

The roles that women play in Taiwanese society have changed over time, as well. For example, modern Taiwanese women are an important part of the working population. In fact, they dominate the labor force in electronics manufacturing. They also make up a large proportion of the textile industry's workers. The range of jobs open to women has broadened over the years, and modern Taiwanese women work in fields including banking, medicine, and the armed forces. But Taiwanese women also face challenges. One of the biggest problems is a large sex industry existing illegally in Taiwan, which employs thousands of child prostitutes. These girls' parents sometimes sell them into prostitution to earn money for the family. Leaders of prostitution rings also trick young women and girls into moving from the countryside into cities, where they are forced into prostitution.

Education

Taiwan's quickly growing economy also offered people better opportunities for education. More than 95 percent of Taiwan's people above the age of 15 are literate—that is, can read and write. All Taiwanese youngsters ages 6 to 15 are required to attend school. During these years, the government pays education costs. Along with teaching students basic academic skills, elementary grades emphasize physical education and moral development. In secondary and vocational school, coursework can lead either to higher education or to a technical profession.

More than 1.25 million students choose to go on to further education after secondary school. They enroll in more than one hundred colleges, universities, and other institutions of higher learning. Graduate divisions offer courses ranging from nuclear science to journalism. Hundreds of foreign students come to Taiwan, where they may take classes in subjects including Chinese culture, medicine, and engineering. The island's largest and oldest university is National Taiwan University in Taipei.

In school in Taipei, some Taiwanese youth study Amoy, a Chinese dialect that has been part of Taiwan's culture for centuries.

The Taiwanese educational system is very effective, and its students are among the most highly ranked in the world. For example, Taiwanese pupils turn in some of the best math and science test scores worldwide. The great pressure placed on Taiwanese young people to excel in school can be overwhelming, however. Suicide rates among students are very high.

Health

Modern Taiwan boasts impressive health statistics. The island was not always so prosperous. After 1949 a variety of changes improved the health of Taiwanese citizens. These changes included higher nutritional standards, better and more readily available medical care, insurance coverage for most of the population, and plentiful quantities of safe drinking water. In 1952, for example, life expectancy on the island was 58 years. That statistic has risen to 76 years—a figure that is comparable to those of larger developed nations. Taiwan's infant death rate has also dropped dramatically. The rate in 1956 was 33 deaths for every 1,000 live births. The rate in modern Taiwan is much lower, with 5.4 babies out of 1,000 dying before the age of one. In mainland China, this rate stands at 27 infant births out of 1,000, while in Japan the figure is 2.8.

Taiwan did face a health challenge in 2003, when a serious outbreak of Severe Acute Respiratory Syndrome (SARS) occurred. While health officials worked to bring the disease under control, the outbreak worsened in May of that year. The nation was not removed from the World Health Organization's list of severely affected countries until July 2003, making it the final nation to come off the list. The nation's rates of other infectious diseases are low, however. For example, HIV/AIDS is rare among Taiwan's citizens.

During the 2003 SARS outbreak in Taiwan, more than 150,000 people were quarantined. Fast action by Taiwanese health officials resulted in laboratory tests that confirmed only 24 cases of SARS.

For many years, Taiwan strongly encouraged family planning to counter the island's high population density. Approximately 71 percent of married Taiwanese women use some form of birth control. Largely as a result of these measures, the rate of the island's population growth is only 0.3 percent. In fact, in modern Taiwan, the population is shrinking quickly enough to concern leaders. According to projections, by the year 2050, the island may be home to only 19.8 million people.

In addition to modern medical practices, some Taiwanese use traditional measures such as herbal cures to heal ailments. Acupuncture is another popular procedure. This ancient Chinese treatment involves the insertion of needles at pressure points in the body. Acupuncture is employed to decrease pain and to cure disease. The continued use of these methods is yet another way in which modern Taiwanese draw on past practices, while also embracing modern advances.

Among other traditional medicinal practices in Taiwan, qigong is a popular exercise. Qigong is believed to benefit health by controlling and strengthening a person's qi. Qi is literally translated as "air" or "breath," and qigong combines certain motions and poses with carefully controlled breathing.

A clerk wraps up a customer's purchase at a **pharmacy for traditional Chinese medicine.** Would you like to read more about the education, health, and daily life of the people of Taiwan? Go to www.vgsbooks.com for links.

CULTURAL LIFE

Like Taiwan's history and people, its culture is closely tied to that of mainland China, while also boasting unique facets. In addition to blending outside influences and local characteristics, Taiwanese life brings together ancient and modern traditions. All together, these elements create a rich and varied cultural scene.

▶ Religion

Taiwan's main religions are Confucianism, Buddhism, and Taoism (also spelled Daoism). All three of these belief systems arrived centuries ago with the island's early Chinese settlers. Most Taiwanese do not practice a single religion in a pure form. Instead, they have adopted elements from each of the island's faiths.

Confucianism is more a code of ethics concerning proper behavior than a religion. It grew from the teachings of Confucius, a philosopher who lived in China in the sixth century B.C. He supported a set of ideals that included respect for authority, strict moral behavior, and

regard for one's ancestors. Many aspects of those beliefs have found their way into everyday Taiwanese life.

Buddhism arose from the teachings of Siddhartha Gautama, who founded the faith in India during the sixth century B.C. The ideals of the Buddha ("Buddha" means the Enlightened One) included the search for enlightenment, giving up worldly possessions, and living a life of virtue and wisdom. These Buddhist values spread rapidly in the years that followed.

Taoism—which, similarly to Confucianism, is a philosophy more than a religion—is derived from the book *Tao Te Ching*. This work is believed to date from the mid-third century B.C. Taoist ideals adopted many features of Buddhism. However, they also grew out of frustration that many Confucians felt toward the strictness of Confucianism. Taoism emphasizes a simple lifestyle, a release from social obligations, and rejection of greed and desire. In addition, Taoism blends with many of the island's folk traditions. These ideas include belief in a supreme being, who is symbolized in Taoist temples by a sacred vessel that burns incense.

Missionary activity in China created a small Christian community on Taiwan among immigrants from the mainland. The Dutch also converted some islanders to Christianity in the seventeenth century, which accounts for a portion of modern-day believers. In all, an estimated 1 million or more Taiwanese identify themselves as Christians. Protestants outnumber Catholics approximately two to one.

◉ Holidays and Festivals

Taiwanese residents celebrate many different holidays and special occasions. Many traditional festivals have their origins in ancient China and are also observed in the PRC. China once used a lunar calendar, based on the cycle of the moon, and some holidays still follow this calendar. The year's most important celebration in both Taiwan and mainland China is the New Year, held on the first day of the lunar year. Preparations and festivities may last for weeks and include special food, decorations, firecrackers, and parades. The ancient Lantern Festival wraps things up on the fifteenth day of the first lunar month.

Another exciting event in Taiwan is the Birthday of Matsu, the traditional folk goddess of the sea. Matsu has many fans in an island nation that has long been home to many sailors and fishers. Taiwan's residents pay their respects to Matsu on the twenty-third day of the third lunar month (usually in April or May). Festivities are particularly large in Peikang, a town near Taiwan's western coast and the site of one of Matsu's most important temples. Throngs of worshipers fill Peikang's streets, stopping at vendors to buy snacks and souvenirs. Folk music, dancing, puppet shows, and other performances entertain the crowds. Processions wind through town to the temple, with people often carrying large statues that represent Matsu herself as well as her fellow gods and goddesses.

Other long-honored celebrations among Taiwanese people include the Mid-Autumn Festival, the Dragon Boat Festival, the Tomb Sweeping Festival, and the Birthday of Confucius (also called Teacher's Day). Paying respects to one's ancestors also figures strongly in traditional Taiwanese religious practices. In ceremonies honoring deceased family members, relatives burn paper replicas of cars, money, and houses. Through this ritual, worshipers believe, the wealth represented by these items may be passed on to bygone ancestors. Also symbolic of local beliefs is Taiwan's abundance of temples, which honor a wide variety of household and regional gods.

Taiwan's indigenous groups celebrate their own festivals, which have no ties to Chinese tradition. The Ami and Rukai peoples hold harvest festivals offering thanks for the season's bounty, highlighted with singing and dancing. The biggest celebration of the year for the Yami people is the Flying Fish Festival. It marks the springtime arrival of these fish, which are a traditional part of the Yami diet.

Official secular (nonreligious) holidays in Taiwan mark important events and honor major figures in the ROC's history. Schools close for many of these special occasions. So do government offices and sometimes other businesses and organizations. One such holiday is Double Ten Day, held on October 10 (10/10). This celebration commemorates

Spectators watch a Dragon Boat Festival race from a bridge in Pitan, Taiwan. The Dragon Boat Festival is dedicated to praying for the ill and the poor.

Young people perform in public for Double Ten Day in Taipei.

the birth of the ROC, which is symbolized by the October 10, 1911, uprising against China's Qing government. The day is filled with festivities such as parades and fireworks, as well as a special speech by Taiwan's president.

Literature

Taiwan's authors draw on a long history of Chinese literature, as well as local influences. The formation of the ROC itself also spurred literary output. During the early years of the ROC, some of the people who followed Chiang Kai-shek from the Chinese mainland to Taiwan went on to write about these turbulent times. One such author was Chu Hsi-ning, a colonel in the Nationalist Army. His anti-Communist fiction discusses the impact of modern life and politics on ordinary people, while also praising traditional values. Chu had two daughters—Chu Tien-wen and Chu Tien-hsin—who also became authors.

Li Ang is a contemporary novelist. Her work focuses on feminist themes and the position of women in Chinese and Taiwanese society. Li's most famous novel is *The Butcher's Wife*, written in 1983. Other Taiwanese fiction writers include Ping Lu, best known for her 1995 novel about Sun Yat-sen, *Walking the Road to the Edge of the Earth*, and Wang Tao. Wang Tao set many of his short stories in his village hometown of Badouzi.

Poetry also holds an important place in the literature of Taiwan. Lin Heng-tai is one of Taiwanese poetry's most important figures. He began writing socially critical poems in the 1940s. A later poet, Bai Chiu, wrote poetry about city life in modern Taiwan. Contemporary Taiwanese poet Chang Shang-hua hosted a radio program in the mid-1990s and recorded readings of her poems accompanied by music.

Other Taiwanese writers keep their native cultures and languages alive through literature. Chung Chao-cheng, for example, writes in Hakka rather than the island's national language of Mandarin Chinese. This preservation effort is sometimes called the *hsiangtu* ("nativist") movement. Huang Chunming is another hsiangtu writer. His short story *The Sandwich Man* was made into a film in 1983.

The National Museum of Taiwanese Literature, located in Tainan, pays tribute to the island's literary output. The museum researches, catalogs, and displays manuscripts and other literary artifacts.

THE BOUNTY OF SPRING

"March was a beautiful month, especially in the big 869 Puyuma Tribal Region in eastern Taiwan. Patches of light green were mixed in the jade green vista. It looked as if someone had carelessly let some water drip on a watercolor painting, then picked it up off the table and blown on it to dry it, leaving pale stains. One need only walk into the mountains amid the jade green to discover that those patches were actually flowers that had lain dormant through the winter and were now blossoming as if there were no tomorrow."

—from "Ginger Road," by Puyuma author Badai

Visual Arts

The government of Taiwan encourages young artists to develop new styles of painting. At the same time, a lot of Taiwanese art uses ideas laid down centuries ago in China. One of Taiwan's most famous painters is Hu Nien-tsu. He combines traditional Chinese forms and styles with more Westernized splashes of bright color. Hu Chi-chung, another well-known artist, creates modern abstract works. An earlier modern figure was the painter Chang Dai-chien, who died in 1983.

Calligraphy (decorative handwriting) is an ancient art form that practitioners continually modernize. Variations on classic shapes are numerous. For example, calligraphers change the thickness, length, and shape of each stroke to produce new and unusual designs.

Traditional Taiwanese handicrafts include carving objects out of wood, bamboo, and stone. Artisans also construct fans of paper, cloth, feathers, and other flexible materials. Kites, bamboo lanterns, and embroidery are other popular creations.

Present-day artists also create many works of porcelain (white ceramic). These potters imitate porcelain makers who worked during the Tang, Ming, and Qing dynasties. In past decades, sales of their work resulted in an economic boom. By the 1990s, ceramic exports were bringing in more than $700 million a year. Worldwide purchases of silk embroideries, wool rugs, and figures made of bronze, brass, and silver also continue to contribute significantly to the Taiwanese economy.

Music, Theater, and Movies

Taiwanese music, too, brings together the new and the old, drawing on Chinese, local, and Western influences. Both classical Chinese and classical Western music have admirers in Taiwan, and traditional styles are taught in the schools. Chinese and Taiwanese music is based on a five-note scale rather than on the eight-note pattern found in Western music. Traditional instruments include the *qin* (a seven-stringed lute), a bamboo flute called a *ti*, and the *san xian* (a three-stringed, guitarlike instrument). Musicians also play gongs, drums, flutes, and horns to perform folk music, which plays an important role in many festivals.

In addition, Taiwan's young people have brought modern music to the island. One popular contemporary star is Chang Hui Mei, who

The Taiwanese boy band **Mayday won the best male vocal performance** Golden Melody award in 2004. The Golden Melody award is an important award in the Chinese-language music industry.

goes by the stage name of A-mei. After releasing her first album in 1996, she became so successful that she's been referred to as the Pride of Taiwan. Another big act is the boy band Fahrenheit, made up of four young men. Each band member represents a season of the year, and each has a distinct image. Their first album came out in 2006. A-mei, Fahrenheit, and other pop stars have gained large audiences in Taiwan, mainland China, and throughout Asia.

Traditional Taiwanese music intertwines with theater in Chinese operas. Drama companies often perform these operas in Taiwanese dialects of Chinese. Dress and facial makeup tell the audience what role each actor and actress plays in the opera. The stage contains very few props, so much of an opera's action depends on the movements and expressions of the players. Other traditional productions include folk dances, sometimes performed atop stilts. Puppet shows using stringed marionettes or large figures made of leather also provide entertainment.

Film is a popular artistic medium in modern Taiwan. At first, the island's moviemakers used the Amoy dialect in their works. Since about 1965, however, most actors speak in Mandarin Chinese. Themes

A **Chinese opera star** gestures dramatically in a performance at the Fu Hsing Dramatic Arts Academy in Taipei.

Hou Hsiao-Hsien received the Akira Kurosawa Award in 2005. It is a lifetime achievement award for film directing, presented at the annual Tokyo International Film Festival.

often involve historical subjects, such as heroes and heroines of China's imperial era. In the early 1980s, Taiwanese films took a different turn with the beginning of New Wave cinema. Movies from this period focused on everyday scenarios and took a realistic look at Taiwanese life and society. Major directors from this period include Edward Yang and Hou Hsiao-Hsien. Hou's work—which has won many awards—is known for being emotional and visually beautiful, while also tackling difficult subjects. For instance, his 1989 film *A City of Sadness* examines a bloody 1947 clash between protesters and Kuomintang troops. Beginning in the 1990s and lasting into the 2000s, a second generation of New Wave directors emerged. These artists are sometimes known as members of the Second New Wave. The best known of the Second New Wave directors—and perhaps of all Taiwanese filmmakers—is Ang Lee (born in 1954). International audiences know Lee from his worldwide releases of movies including *Crouching Tiger, Hidden Dragon* (2000), *Hulk* (2003), and *Brokeback Mountain* (2005).

Food

Taiwan has a rich and varied cuisine. Its main ingredients are rice, pork, and soy products (such as soy sauce and tofu). Noodle dishes and soups featuring pork and vegetables are standard fare. Pork is the usual filling for the popular *ba wan,* an extra-large dumpling that is an island favorite. Steamed and fried buns filled with meat are also common. Seafood makes up a significant part of the Taiwanese diet, as well. Shrimp, fish, and other types of seafood may be eaten fried, steamed, or grilled. Taiwanese chefs spice up these dishes with a wide variety of flavorings. These seasonings include chili peppers, soy sauce, sesame oil, ginger, and pickled radishes. And for dessert, a healthy choice is the fresh fruit that flourishes in the island's warm weather. Prepared sweets such as custards and pastries are also favorite ways to end a meal.

In addition to islandwide dishes, many cities have their own specialties. Hsinchu is known for its soup with pork meatballs, while Taichung's signature delicacy is the suncake—a flaky, filled pastry. Night markets are also popular. They open after sundown in cities around Taiwan and serve up a wide range of *xiaochi,* or "small eats."

This **night market stand** in Taichung sells salads.

GREEN ONION PANCAKES

These tasty fried rounds are a favorite snack at Taiwan's night markets.

3 cups flour, plus a little extra

1 cup hot water

¼ cup soy sauce

¼ cup rice wine vinegar

1 teaspoon minced fresh ginger

1 teaspoon red pepper flakes (optional)

2 teaspoons sesame oil

1 teaspoon salt

1 teaspoon black pepper

½ bunch green onion or scallion tops, sliced thinly

½ cup peanut oil

1. Mix flour and water in a large bowl. The dough will be dry. On a lightly floured countertop, use lightly floured hands to knead dough for about 10 minutes, until smooth. Roll into a ball and place in a clean bowl. Cover and let sit for 30 minutes.

2. Combine soy sauce, vinegar, ginger, and red pepper flakes (if desired) in a bowl to make dipping sauce.

3. Place sesame oil, salt and pepper, and green onions in three separate small bowls. Shape dough into a long rope about 1-inch thick. Cut into pieces about 1½ inches long.

4. Flatten each piece of dough with a rolling pin to form a ⅛-inch-thick circle. Using a pastry brush or your fingers, lightly brush the top of the circle with sesame oil. Sprinkle with a pinch of salt and pepper and about ½ teaspoon of scallions.

5. Fold over one edge of the circle, and use your fingers to roll the seasoned dough up toward the opposite edge of the circle. You should end up with a small, short rope, with the seasoning inside. Pinch the rope closed, and coil it into a snail shape. Pinch the ends again, and use the rolling pin to flatten the dough into a small pancake. Repeat with remaining dough.

6. Heat peanut oil in a shallow frying pan over medium high heat. Carefully place three or four pancakes in the oil and fry about 1 minute, or until golden brown on the bottom. Use a spatula to flip pancakes and cook another 45 seconds. Remove and drain on paper towels. Repeat with remaining pancakes. Serve hot with dipping sauce.

Serves 6 to 8

These portable snacks include grilled squid on a stick, thin green onion pancakes, rice balls, sausages, and salad.

The Sporting Life

Taiwanese schools encourage physical fitness, and sports are popular throughout the island. In Olympic competitions, Taiwanese athletes excel at track and field, archery, table tennis, tae-kwondo, and weight lifting. Team members have brought home medals in all of these sports.

Since 1984 Taiwanese athletes have participated in the Olympics as part of "Chinese Taipei." This special designation represents a compromise with the PRC that allows both China and Taiwan to compete as separate teams.

In addition to the Olympics and to the multinational Asian Games, Taiwanese competitors participate in many local sporting events. Basketball, track and field, and soccer are widely popular. Professional golfers from Taiwan are prominent in international tournaments. Baseball is also a leading sport, with great success being achieved by little leaguers. Taiwanese teams have won many titles in the Little League World Series, which involves teams from around the globe.

Taiwanese soccer player Li Chia-Lun *(front)* blocks a Japanese player in a **women's semi-final match at the Asian Games.**

THE ECONOMY

During the last half of the twentieth century, Taiwan's industrialization and economic growth took place so rapidly that it is often called the Taiwan Miracle. As a result of this miracle, modern Taiwanese have a high standard of living. They also have one of the best gross national incomes (GNI) per capita in the world. (GNI is a measure of the income a nation earns in a year, compared to its population.) The ROC also maintains a respected place among the globe's economies.

The miracle replaced an economy that had been largely agricultural until 1949. Before then, most people worked as farmers. Many of the industries that did already exist had been heavily bombed during World War II. The transition to a more industrial economy began in the 1950s with a series of four-year economic programs. These plans used large amounts of U.S. aid to develop manufacturing on a large scale. But the programs also recognized agriculture's importance. The first manufacturing centers focused on processing crops, such as sugarcane and pineapples. As a result, Taiwan has maintained a high rate of agricultural growth along with its industrial expansion.

In 1965, for the first time, industry contributed more than agriculture did to the gross national product (GNP, the total value of goods and services produced within a country in one year). Taiwan's GNP growth had reached about 6 percent a year by the mid-1990s. This rate placed Taiwan among the "East Asian Tigers"—fast-growing regional nations that became international manufacturing and export centers.

Taiwan's progress slowed somewhat in the 2000s but did continue, even as many other Asian economies suffered severe setbacks. In 2002 the island's economy took another important step. That year, after years of negotiation, Taiwan joined the World Trade Organization (WTO). Taiwan became a WTO member under the name Chinese Taipei.

Services and Trade

Taiwan's economy has rapidly grown in the service sector. Services include banking, insurance, health care, and retail sales. Tourism is also part of the service sector, and more than 2 million people visit Taiwan in an average year.

The rapid rise in the nation's income per person in the late twentieth century promoted growth in these fields. In turn, as demand for better services increased, more Taiwanese workers switched from manual labor to service-related jobs. In modern Taiwan, services account for nearly 70 percent of the nation's gross domestic product, or GDP. (Similar to GNP, GDP is a measure of the total annual value of goods and services produced by a nation's citizens.) Services also occupy approximately 55 percent of Taiwanese workers.

Exports also remain critical to Taiwan's economy. The island's main trading partners are the United States, Hong Kong, Japan, and Germany. Most of the nation's imports come from Japan, the United States, South Korea, and Germany. Trade with the PRC also began to increase during the 1990s. Taiwan's healthy export market has given it a large trade surplus, meaning that Taiwanese companies earn more money from exports than the Taiwanese people spend on foreign goods.

TRADE WINDS

Taiwan's heavy dependence on foreign trade leaves it vulnerable to negative trends and shifts in the global market. For example, the Taiwanese economy suffered after the September 11, 2001, terrorist attacks on the United States—one of the island's largest trade partners. In an attempt to minimize this danger, the island's economic planners work to broaden the nation's range of export products. As part of this effort, Taiwan economists are also seeking a wider range of nations with which to trade.

Industry

Taiwan's success at developing a strong industrial sector is clear from the frequent presence of the "Made in Taiwan" label on products throughout the world. By 1965 Taiwan had become a leading exporter of light industrial products, such as textiles, plastics, and small appliances.

In the late 1980s, Taiwan's economic planners engineered a major manufacturing transition. They outlined a shift away from producing items that required mostly manual labor. In doing so, these planners laid the groundwork for the country's factories to assemble high-tech products. Taiwan became

Most electronics made in Taiwan are assembled in Hsinchu. More than three hundred high-tech companies have facilities there.

a leading supplier of computer hardware, precision instruments, airplane machinery, and sophisticated scientific and engineering equipment.

This industrial shift required fewer workers. Nevertheless, Taiwan's manufacturing sector remains heavily dependent on the island's skilled labor force. In the 2000s, more than 35 percent of the working population is involved in producing factory-made items. Computers and office machines are the island's most valuable exports. But factories in Taiwan also produce goods including glass, calculators, clothing, shoes, sporting goods, tires, toys, and cement. Laborers at steel and aluminum plants manufacture machine tools and electrical equipment. All together, industrial production makes up approximately 20 percent of Taiwan's GDP.

Agriculture

Agriculture in Taiwan has gone through a number of different phases. Before 1949, for example, landlords owned most of the island's farmable land. Tenant farmers lived in mud huts and gave more than half of their crops to the landlords. In keeping with Sun Yat-sen's teachings, however, the new ROC government enacted land reform. As part of these reforms, many former landlords became the heads of giant corporations. In addition, more than 90 percent of modern Taiwanese farmers own the land that they cultivate.

Agriculture remained the backbone of Taiwan's economy until the early 1960s. But in the subsequent decades, more and more farm workers—especially women—left the fields. They moved to large cities to earn the higher wages that big businesses offered. The agricultural sector in present-day Taiwan only accounts for about 2 percent of the island's GDP and employs between 5 and 10 percent of the total labor force.

Only about 25 percent of Taiwan's land is arable (able to be farmed), and most of this area lies on the western coastal plain. Because the island's soil is not naturally fertile, farmers use a variety of fertilizers to add valuable nutrients to the land. Modern machinery, improved irrigation, pesticides (substances that kill insects and other pests), and better seeds have also increased agricultural production.

Taiwan is among the world's largest exporters of asparagus, which grows along the island's seashores and rivers. In addition, workers harvest three crops of rice each year. This yield is enough to feed the population and also leave a surplus for export. Terracing—cutting level

Taiwanese workers plant rice.

Small **terraced fields** lie nestled between mountains. The indigenous Rukai living in the Maolin Scenic Area cultivate rice and other crops here.

strips into the hillsides to increase the amount of farmable land—also helps farmers keep up with local food demands. Along with asparagus and rice, principal Taiwanese crops are sugarcane, sweet potatoes, mushrooms, and other vegetables. Citrus fruit, pineapples, and bananas are also important products.

Livestock—especially water buffalo—once played an important role as labor animals in Taiwan. Mechanized farming methods have made the use of draft (load-pulling) animals less common. Nevertheless, Taiwanese farmers still raise pigs, goats, chickens, and ducks for food.

Forestry and Fishing

Taiwan's forests are one of its few abundant natural resources. Woodlands cover more than half of the island's territory, mostly in its mountainous center. Cedar, hemlock, and oak are among Taiwan's most valuable trees. Bamboo and camphor also contribute to the economy. Trees provide lumber for construction as well as firewood for fuel. While the government encourages improvements in logging methods, it also actively sponsors reforestation efforts on the island. In coastal areas, the forest forms a barrier against the damaging winds of typhoons.

Taiwan's fishing industry operates in both the waters surrounding the island and those within Taiwan. Using modern boats and

Fishing boats crowd the **small port city of Suao** in Taiwan.

up-to-date equipment, deepsea and shoreline fishers ply the ocean. Saltwater catches include tuna, shrimp, and mackerel. Inland, fish-breeding farms specialize in raising carp, eels, and other freshwater fish for local markets. Together, forestry and fishing contribute approximately 2 percent to Taiwan's GDP.

Transportation and Energy

Taiwan has an extensive network of overland transportation routes. Railways—many of them built by businesses to move their goods— connect all the major cities, ports, and industrial zones. Trains also carry passengers around Taiwan. A rail system that circles the entire island was completed in 1991. All together, more than 1,400 miles (2,253 km) of track crisscross the island.

Taiwan also boasts a large network of roads and highways, with more than 23,000 miles (37,015 km) of roads, most of which are paved. An expressway connects Taipei to Kaohsiung, and another freeway links cities along the western coast. Approximately one-fifth of Taiwanese residents own

BUTTERFLY LANE

In 2007 Taiwan's government sealed off 1,800 feet (549 m) of a highway to protect migrating milkweed butterflies. These butterflies migrate 180 miles (290 km) from the northern part of the island to the southern part to escape winter cold. Nets installed along the highway and special ultraviolet lights placed on an overpass help them cross the road safely.

High-speed train service between Taipei and Kaohsiung started in 2007. It shortens the travel time between the two cities from more than four hours to only ninety minutes.

cars, and the island's bus services also aid in daily travel. Intercity electric railways provide additional transportation, and Taipei has had its own subway system since 1996. Some people also rely on more traditional means such as walking or bicycling to travel from place to place.

China Airlines flies into the Chiang Kai-shek International Airport in Taoyuan near Taipei. The airline also offers domestic flights to more than one dozen smaller airports on the island. Chiang Kai-shek International Airport opened a second passenger terminal in 2000. This addition—along with other expansions and modifications—is expected to give the airport a capacity of 14 million more passengers per year by 2010.

Taiwan lacks significant natural sources of fossil fuel, such as coal or oil. As a result, it relies heavily on hydroelectric power and thermal plants to provide energy for industry. The island also imports some crude oil, which its own refineries convert into usable fuel. In addition, Taiwan operates several nuclear power plants, which produce power by controlling nuclear chemical reactions.

The island of Taiwan has six international ports, with the main two located at Kaohsiung and Keelung. In the past decades, facilities for building, repairing, and berthing ships in those ports have been modernized and expanded.

◉ Media and Communications

When seeking information and entertainment, Taiwan residents have a wide number of media sources to choose from. The ROC produces more than four hundred newspapers, as well as more than four thousand magazines and other periodicals. Taiwanese can also tune in to more than one hundred radio stations, or watch public, broadcast, or cable television.

More than 13 million people in Taiwan subscribe to traditional, land-line telephone service. Many others use mobile phones to com-

Apple Daily, a newspaper from Hong Kong, China, launched a Taiwanese edition in 2003. To catch up on the daily news in Taiwan and to learn more about its economy, go to www.vgsbooks.com for links.

municate. In addition, approximately 70 percent of Taiwanese households have Internet connections. Many Internet cafes in Taipei and other large cities also give people the chance to get online.

The Future

Since entering the world arena in 1949, Taiwan has struggled to find its place in international affairs. For three decades, the ROC fought for its claim to authority over China. In the 1970s, much of the international community rejected that claim. In the 1980s, a strong economy brought the Taiwanese greater prosperity and also a larger share of the global market. In the 1990s, many Taiwanese gave up the claim of power over China. Meanwhile, the development of sophisticated export products showed the island's ability to adapt to changing times.

By the early 2000s, Taiwan had nearly 24 million registered mobile phone subscribers—meaning that there were more subscribers than residents on the island. This ratio of 1,062 phones to 1,000 people gave Taiwan the highest such rate in the world.

Taiwan has also advanced politically. Taiwan's political structure is less restricted and less centralized than when Chiang Kai-shek ran the government. It has broadened to include more native Taiwanese and has legalized non-Kuomintang political parties. Then, with the election of Chen Shui-bian in 2000, the Kuomintang lost its long-held dominance over the island's administration.

Despite these important changes, many old issues remain unresolved in the 2000s. Scandal and corruption still plague the island's politics. In addition, Taiwan's relationship with mainland China remains tense. Chinese leaders continue to see Taiwan as a province of the PRC. Taiwanese themselves are divided on whether reunification with China, full independence, or some alternative solution is best for Taiwan and its people. More than once, the dispute has threatened to erupt into armed conflict. Supporters of each solution—on both sides of the Taiwan Strait—continue to vocalize their positions, sometimes aggressively. And while modern economic ties between China and Taiwan bring them into closer contact and encourage greater stability, a permanent agreement remains elusive. Whatever else the future brings, solving this problem will remain among the largest challenges facing Taiwan, the beautiful island.

Timeline

CA. 28,000 B.C.	Prehistoric communities exist on Taiwan.
500s B.C.	Siddhartha Gautama founds Buddhism.
A.D. 600s	Tang dynasty expeditions travel to what will later become Taiwan.
960-1279	The Song dynasty rules China, and exploration to Taiwan continues.
1279	Kublai Khan founds the Yuan dynasty.
1292	Mongol leaders send an expedition to Taiwan. They send another in 1297.
1368	The Ming dynasty takes over from the Mongols.
1589	Ming officials provide Chinese merchants with trading licenses that enable them to do business in Taiwan. They issue more in 1593.
1609	Japanese forces attempt to take control of Taiwan. They try again in 1616. Both attempts fail.
1622	The Dutch East India Company oversees a military outpost on the Penghu Islands.
1626	Spanish settlers build forts on Taiwan.
1644	The Manchu set up the Qing dynasty.
1661	Zheng Chenggong flees mainland China to Taiwan.
1684	The Qing dynasty makes Taiwan an administrative unit of the Chinese province of Fujian.
1700s	Rebellions against Taiwan's Qing rulers increase.
CA.1880	Liu Mingchuan becomes Taiwan's governor.
1885	Taiwan becomes a province of China. Taipei becomes Taiwan's capital city.
1895	The Treaty of Shimonoseki transfers control of Taiwan from China to Japan.
1911	An October 10 revolt against the Qing government brings about the beginning of the Republic of China (ROC).
1921	The Chinese Communist Party (CCP) is formed on mainland China.
1925	Sun Yat-sen dies, and Chiang Kai-shek becomes the ROC's leader.
1939-1945	World War II takes place. Allied forces heavily bomb Taiwan.

1949   Mao Zedong establishes the People's Republic of China
        (PRC) on mainland China. Chiang Kai-shek and nearly three mil-
        lion of his soldiers and followers leave for Taiwan. Taipei becomes
        the ROC's capital. Chiang institutes martial law.

1954   The United States and the ROC sign a mutual defense treaty. The First
        Taiwan Strait Crisis breaks out.

1958   The Second Taiwan Strait Crisis erupts.

1970s   Taiwan's rapid economic growth grants its people one of the highest standards
        of living in Asia.

1971   The ROC is replaced by the PRC in the General Assembly of the United Nations.

1975   Chiang Kai-shek dies.

1978   Chiang Kai-shek's son Chiang Ching-kou becomes Taiwan's leader.

1986   Taiwanese-born Lee Yuan T. wins a Nobel Prize in Chemistry.

1987   Chiang Ching-kou lifts martial law.

1988   Lee Teng-hui becomes Taiwan's first Hakka president.

1995   The Third Taiwan Strait Crisis takes place.

1996   Voters choose Lee Teng-hui as president in Taiwan's first direct presidential election.

1999   The Chi-Chi earthquake kills more than 2,400 people in central Taiwan.

2000   Taiwanese elect Chen Shui-bian, making him the first non-Kuomintang president of
        Taiwan.

2002   Taiwan becomes a member of the World Trade Organization.

2003   Taiwan has an outbreak of Severe Acute Respiratory Syndrome (SARS).

2004   Chen Shui-bian and his vice president, Annette Lu, are shot while campaigning in
        Tainan. They are reelected the next day. The Taipei 101 building opens to the public.

2005   The PRC passes an anti-secession law, blocking Taiwanese independence.

2006   Filmmaker Ang Lee wins a best director Academy Award for his movie *Brokeback
        Mountain*.

2007   High-speed train service begins between Taipei and Kaohsiung.

COUNTRY NAME Republic of China, or Taiwan

AREA 13,969 square miles (36,180 sq. km)

MAIN LANDFORMS Central Mountain Range, western plain, eastern coastal strip

HIGHEST POINT Yu Shan (also called Jade Mountain), 13,113 feet (3,997 m) above sea level

MAJOR RIVERS Choshui River, Hsintien River, Keelung River, Lower Tanshui River, Tsengwen River

ANIMALS apes, black bears, deer, Formosan macaques, Formosan serows, kingfishers, larks, pangolins, panthers, wild boars

CAPITAL CITY Taipei

OTHER MAJOR CITIES Kaohsiung, Taichung, Tainan, Makung

OFFICIAL LANGUAGE Mandarin Chinese

MONETARY UNIT New Taiwan dollar (TWD). 100 cents = 1 New Taiwan dollar.

TAIWAN CURRENCY

The New Taiwan dollar has been the ROC's official currency since 1949, when it replaced the Old Taiwan dollar. The currency is called the yuan in Mandarin Chinese and is known more casually as the *kuai* in Mandarin or *kho* in Taiwanese dialects. Paper currency is issued in denominations of one hundred, two hundred, five hundred, one thousand, and two thousand dollars. Banknotes display portraits of historical figures, important architecture, regional wildlife, and other representations of Taiwan. Coins are minted in values of one-half dollar (although these coins are very rarely used), and one, five, ten, twenty, and fifty dollars. Most of them show historical figures such as Chiang Kai-shek and Sun Yat-sen.

Adopted in 1928, the Taiwanese flag is mostly red, with a dark blue rectangle in the upper-left quadrant. Inside the blue rectangle lies a white sun with twelve triangular rays. The colors of the flag represent Sun Yat-sen's Three Principles of the People. Red stands for nationalism, blue for democracy, and white for the livelihood of the people. The sun and its rays represent forward progress.

Flag

The Republic of China's national anthem was unofficially chosen in the 1930s and formally adopted in 1943. Several Kuomintang members cooperated in writing the lyrics, which were based upon a speech by Sun Yat-sen. Cheng Mao-Yun composed the anthem's music.

Not all English translations of Taiwan's anthem—which is sometimes casually called "San Min Chu-I" or "Three Principles of the People"—are alike. One version follows.

National Anthem

San Min Chu-I,
Our aim shall be:
To found a free land,
World peace be our stand.
Lead on, comrades, vanguards ye are.
Hold fast your aim, by sun and star.
Be earnest and brave, your country to save.
One heart, one soul, one mind, one goal!

 Would you like to hear Taiwan's national anthem? You can do that by going to www.vgsbooks.com for a link.

Famous People

Taiwanese names consist of a family name and a personal name. For example, Sun Yat-sen is from the Sun family, and his personal name is Yat-sen. The following Taiwanese names are written in the traditional order, with family name first.

CHANG HUI MEI (b. 1972) Born in eastern Taiwan, Chang is one of her country's biggest and brightest musical stars. Better known to her many fans as A-mei, she is a member of the Puyuma ethnic group. She broke into show business in her early twenties, winning a Taiwanese talent show competition and later signing a recording contract. She released her debut album in 1996, and it became an almost instant hit. A-mei's career has gone through some rough patches—such as in 2000, when her singing of the Republic of China's national anthem at Chen Shui-bian's inauguration ceremonies upset PRC officials. However, she remains a huge pop star in Taiwan and beyond.

CHEN SHIH-HSIN (b. 1978) Chen Shih-Hsin began practicing the martial art of taekwondo at age five. She quickly proved herself a talented competitor, becoming the sport's world champion in 1994 and winning a second world championship two years later. In 2001 she was named among Taiwan's Ten Outstanding Young Persons for that year. And in 2004, she won the gold medal in her taekwondo weight range at the Summer Olympics in Athens, Greece. The victory made Chen the first Taiwan-born winner of Olympic gold. (Just minutes later, Chu Mu Yen became Taiwan's second gold medal winner in his taekwondo event.) Following her Olympic victory, Chen went on to study at Taipei Physical Education College.

CHIANG KAI-SHEK (1887–1975) Born in Xikou, in mainland China, Chiang Kai-shek joined the military as a young man. He studied at two military academies, and in 1911 he led soldiers in the fight to overthrow the Qing government. Following the revolution, he became a founding member of the Kuomintang and a close associate of Sun Yat-sen. In 1924 Sun appointed Chiang head of the Whampoa Military Academy, a Kuomintang-led training institution in Guangzhou. After Sun's death the next year, Chiang succeeded him as head of the Kuomintang. He continued the Nationalists' struggle against the Communists for control of China, but in 1949 the Communists won and Chiang fled to Taiwan. There he served as ROC president for more than twenty years. His wife, Soong May-ling (often called Madame Chiang Kai-shek), also played a significant role in Taiwanese politics. When Chiang died at the age of eighty-seven, the island was plunged into mourning.

CHUNG CHAO-CHENG (b. 1925) Chung Chao-cheng is a prominent Hakka author. He worked as a schoolteacher for four decades. At the same time, he began writing novels at the age of twenty. Much of his writing focuses on Hakka life and culture, as well as Taiwanese rural life. He has authored more than twenty novels, as well as several volumes of short stories. He says of his work in the Hakka language, "We are pioneers of Taiwanese literature, a literature with unique characteristics." Chung has won a number of awards and was also appointed as an adviser to President Chen Shui-bian in 2000.

LEE ANG (b. 1954) Lee Ang (known in the West as Ang Lee) was born in Chaojhou in southern Taiwan. He went to college at the National Arts School (which later became the National Taiwan University of Arts). Lee got his big break in 1990 when two of his screenplays won first and second place in a Taiwanese competition. The results were Lee's films *Pushing Hands* (1992) and *The Wedding Banquet* (1993). Both focused on the lives of Taiwanese immigrants to the United States and were popular with the critics, and the second won many awards. Since then, Lee has directed many films, including *Sense and Sensibility* (1995), *Crouching Tiger, Hidden Dragon* (2000), and *Hulk* (2003). In 2006 he won the Academy Award for best direction for *Brokeback Mountain*, becoming the first Asian filmmaker to receive the honor.

LEE YUAN T. (b. 1936) Born in Hsinchu, Lee Yuan T. was a talented young athlete and also a promising student. Deciding to pursue a career in science, he earned university degrees in Taiwan and the United States. Lee worked and taught at several U.S. universities. His research of chemical reactions won him the 1986 Nobel Prize in Chemistry (sharing the award with Dudley R. Herschbach and John C. Polanyi)—making him the first Taiwan-born Nobel winner. In 1994 Lee returned to Taiwan. He has participated in Taiwanese committees on education, community, and relations with mainland China.

SHIH SHU-TUAN (b. 1952) Born in Lukang in western Taiwan, feminist novelist Shih Shu-tuan is better known by her pen name, Li Ang. She attended Chinese Culture University in Taipei, earning her bachelor degree in philosophy in 1974. She also studied in the United States. She went on to write many novels and short stories. Her best-known work is her 1983 novella *The Butcher's Wife*, describing a woman who kills her abusive husband. In 1985 her novel *Dark Night* was one of the top ten best-selling books in Taiwan, and both this book and *The Butcher's Wife* were made into films. Along with her success, however, Li Ang has attracted controversy, as her work is often critical of traditional Taiwanese and Chinese culture.

FORT ZEELANDIA, TAINAN Dating back to the 1600s, Fort Zeelandia was built by Dutch merchants and settlers in Taiwan. In modern times, history buffs can explore the remains of the old stone structure as well as the surrounding grounds. Fort Zeelandia is also known as Anping Fort.

KENTING NATIONAL PARK Located at Taiwan's southern tip, this protected area covers more than 120 square miles (311 sq. km) of land and water. Within this space lie mountains, sandy beaches, rivers, lakes, cliffs, and precious coral reefs. With its rich variety of ecosystems, the park is a habitat for many different kinds of wildlife, from birds, frogs, and mammals to sea turtles and more than one thousand species of fish.

LONGSHAN TEMPLE, TAIPEI Settlers from mainland China originally built this Buddhist temple in western Taipei in the early 1700s. Damaged and destroyed on multiple occasions over the years by earthquakes, typhoons, and war, the temple has been rebuilt many times. With its beautiful traditional architecture and its rich symbolism, the temple remains one of Taiwan's most famous religious sites.

NATIONAL PALACE MUSEUM, TAIPEI This massive museum in Taiwan's capital houses more than 700,000 artifacts of Chinese and Taiwanese art and culture—making it among the largest such collections in the world.

SHILIN NIGHT MARKET, TAIPEI There are more than two dozen night markets in Taiwan, but Shilin is the largest and best-known of these nighttime attractions. The market is located on the site of a onetime day market that opened in 1909, and in modern Taipei it draws hundreds of visitors from the city and beyond. Vendors serve up hot and cold snacks such as pork dumplings, oyster omelets, and fried chicken.

TAROKO GORGE This natural wonder is located near the city of Hualien, on Taiwan's central eastern coast, and is a dramatic rift through the mountains of the region. Visitors follow hiking trails in the gorge, from which they can view waterfalls and monasteries, visit tea houses, and maybe even catch a glimpse of wild monkeys.

Buddhism: a religion founded in India by the monk Siddhartha Gautama (the Buddha, or the Enlightened One) in the 500s B.C. Buddhism gained a following in China and Taiwan between the third and sixth centuries A.D. Some of Buddhism's central ideas are the search for enlightenment, freedom from the desire for worldly things, and living a life of virtue and wisdom.

Communism: a political and economic model based on the idea of common, rather than private, property. In a Communist system, the government controls resources and distributes them equally among citizens.

Confucianism: a system of beliefs about proper actions, based on the teachings of the philosopher Confucius, who emphasized the necessity of proper conduct in all aspects of life. Confucianism also arranges society into rigid classes.

dynasty: a ruling family. Within dynasties, power is usually handed down from fathers to sons, and one dynasty may remain in control for hundreds of years.

Kuomintang: formed by Sun Yat-sen to establish a Chinese republic (a political system without a monarch), the Kuomintang became the ROC's dominant political party in 1949 and remained so for nearly half a century.

nationalism: a philosophy or ideal valuing strong loyalty to one's own nation before all others. Nationalism also emphasizes the promotion and preservation of national culture and dedication to fulfilling the nation's needs.

propaganda: ideas or information that is spread—often by a government—to enforce a desired mindset and to strengthen the control of one party or system

Taoism: a system of thought that appeared around the fourth century B.C. A central idea of Taoism is following the Tao, or the Way, which can be defined as nature, the universe, or reality. Taoism focuses on a simple, harmonious life. Its central text, the *Tao Te Ching*, was written by Lao-tzu.

United Nations: an international organization formed at the end of World War II in 1945 to help handle global disputes. The United Nations replaced a similar, earlier group known as the League of Nations.

Western: a geographic and political term that usually refers to the politics, culture, and history of the United States and Europe

Selected Bibliography

Balcom, John, and Yingtsih Balcom, eds. *Indigenous Writers of Taiwan: An Anthology of Stories, Essays, and Poems.* John Balcom, trans. New York: Columbia University Press, 2005.
This collection presents a range of works by indigenous Taiwanese authors.

Bates, Chris, and Ling-li Bates. *Culture Shock! Taiwan: A Survival Guide to Customs and Etiquette.* Portland, OR: Graphic Arts Center Publishing, 2005.
This book offers an overview of Taiwanese culture and society.

Carver, Ann C., and Sung-Shen Yvonne Chang, eds. *Bamboo Shoots after the Rain: Contemporary Stories by Women Writers of Taiwan.* New York: Feminist Press at the City University of New York, 1990.
This anthology presents the work of Taiwanese female authors.

Davison, Gary Marvin, and Barbara E. Reed. *Culture and Customs of Taiwan.* Westport, CT: Greenwood Press, 1998.
This volume covers Taiwanese cultural life, both traditional and modern.

Europa World Yearbook, 2006. Vol. II. London: Europa Publications, 2006.
Covering the Republic of China's recent history, economy, and government, this annual publication also provides a wealth of statistics on population, employment, trade, and more.

Jordan, David K, Andrew D. Morris, and Marc L. Moskowitz, ed. *The Minor Arts of Daily Life: Popular Culture in Taiwan.* Westport, CT: Greenwood Press, 1998.
This volume brings together information on many cultural aspects of Taiwanese life, from religion to television to night markets.

Li Chien-lang. *Tour of Historical Sites of Taiwan.* Taipei, Taiwan: Tourism Bureau, Republic of China, 1996.
This slim book gives an overview of Taiwan's major historical places.

Manthorpe, Jonathan. *Forbidden Nation: A History of Taiwan.* New York: Palgrave Macmillan, 2005.
This book examines Taiwan's history up to present times.

New York Times Company. *The New York Times on the Web.* 2007.
http://www.nytimes.com (February 8, 2007).
This online version of the newspaper offers current news stories along with an archive of articles on Taiwan.

"PRB 2006 World Population Data Sheet." *Population Reference Bureau (PRB).* 2006.
http://www.prb.org (February 8, 2007).
This annual statistics sheet provides a wealth of data on Taiwan's population, birth and death rates, fertility rate, infant mortality rate, and other useful demographic information.

Roy, Denny. *Taiwan: A Political History.* **Ithaca, NY: Cornell University Press, 2003.**
This title examines Taiwan's history through the often stormy politics that have surrounded the island.

Storey, Robert. *Taiwan.* **Oakland, CA: Lonely Planet Publications, 2001.**
This book provides information on Taiwanese history, culture, sights to see, and more.

Tourism Bureau, Republic of China. *Performing Folk Arts and Handicrafts in Taiwan.* **Taipei, Taiwan: Tourism Bureau, Republic of China, 1996.**
This book examines traditional crafts and artworks in Taiwan.

Turner, Barry, ed. *The Statesman's Yearbook: The Politics, Cultures, and Economies of the World, 2007.* **New York: Macmillan Press, 2006.**
This resource provides concise information on Taiwan's history, climate, government, economy, and culture, including relevant statistics.

Wieman, Earl. *Festivals in Taiwan.* **Taipei, Taiwan: Tourism Bureau, Ministry of Transportation and Communications, Republic of China, 1997.**
This book gives readers a look at major Taiwanese holidays and festivals.

BBC News—Asia-Pacific
http://news.bbc.co.uk/2/hi/asia-pacific/default.stm
This news site provides a range of up-to-date information and archived articles about Taiwan.

Behnke, Alison. *China in Pictures*. Minneapolis: Lerner Publications Company, 2003.
This book presents an introduction to China, Taiwan's neighbor and Taiwan's political opponent since 1949.

CIA—The World Factbook—Taiwan
https://www.cia.gov/cia/publications/factbook/geos/tw.html
This site offers an overview of Taiwan's geography, demographics, and other characteristics.

CNN.com International—Asia
http://edition.cnn.com/ASIA/
Check CNN for current events and breaking news about Taiwan, as well as a searchable archive of older articles.

Folk Stories of Taiwan
http://www.taiwandc.org/folk.htm
Visit this site to read a selection of traditional folktales from Taiwan, including a Shao story about Sun Moon Lake.

Green, Robert. *Taiwan*. San Diego: Greenhaven Press, 2004.
This book focuses on the many transitions that Taiwan has been through in its history and how those transitions affect modern Taiwan and its people.

———*Taiwan*. San Diego: Lucent Books, 2001.
From the Nations in Transition series, this title examines Taiwan and its ever-evolving relationship with China.

Hsiao-Lan Hu, and William Cully Allen. *Taoism*. Philadelphia: Chelsea House, 2005.
Learn more about Taoism, a belief system followed by some Taiwanese.

Kort, Michael G. *The Handbook of East Asia*. Minneapolis: Twenty-First Century Books, 2006.
This volume presents profiles of East Asia's nations, including Taiwan, examining culture, people, government, and more.

Lonely Planet—Taiwan
http://www.lonelyplanet.com/worldguide/destinations/asia/taiwan/
Designed for travelers, this site provides information on Taiwanese history, sights to see, and more.

Macdonald, Phil. *National Geographic Traveler: Taiwan*. Washington, D.C.: National Geographic Society, 2004.
Browse this book for information about visiting Taiwan and its attractions, from natural wonders to historic sites.

Sherman, Josepha. *The Cold War*. Minneapolis: Lerner Publications Company, 2004.
The Cold War affected Taiwan, along with many other nations of Asia and the world. Read this book to learn more about this unique conflict.

vgsbooks.com
http://www.vgsbooks.com
Visit vgsbooks.com, the homepage of the Visual Geography Series®. You can get linked to all sorts of useful on-line information, including geographical, historical, demographic, cultural, and economic websites. The vgsbooks.com site is a great resource for late-breaking news and statistics.

Wilkinson, Philip. *Buddhism*. New York: Dorling Kindersley, 2003.
This title provides an introduction to Buddhism, one of Taiwan's major faiths.

Williams, Barbara. *World War II : Pacific*. Minneapolis: Twenty-First Century Books, 2005.
This comprehensive account details Pacific Ocean battles in World War II.

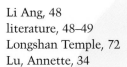

Captions for photos appearing on cover and chapter openers:

Cover: Pagodalike rain shelters offer tourists breathtaking views of Hsitou Forest Recreation Area in Taiwan.

pp. 4–5 Since 2004 the skyscraper Taipei 101 has dominated the horizon of Taipei, the capital of Taiwan.

pp. 8–9 The port city of Kaohsiung bustles with activity.

pp. 18–19 These statues, representing four of the twelve signs of the Chinese zodiac, were created during the Tang dynasty. These zodiac signs are still important symbols in modern Taiwan.

pp. 36–37 Two young women model the traditional clothing of the indigenous Ami for tourists.

pp. 44–45 Paper lanterns adorn the Lungshan Temple in Taipei for the annual Lantern Festival. It is celebrated on the fifteenth day of the first lunar month of the Chinese New Year.

Photo Acknowledgments

© Jeremy Woodhouse/The Image Bank/Getty Images, pp. 4–5; © XNR Productions, pp. 6, 10; © Helene Rogers/Art Directors, pp. 8–9, 17, 60, 62; © Henry Westheim Photography/Alamy, p. 11; © STR/AFP/Getty Images, p. 13; © Patrick Lin/AFP/Getty Images, pp. 14, 41, 48, 50; © Louie Psihoyos/Science Faction/Getty Images, p. 16; © Werner Forman/Art Resource, NY, pp. 18–19; © The Granger Collection, New York, p. 21; Library of Congress, pp. 25 (top, LC-USZ62-5972), 29 (LC-USZ62-069155); © Hulton Archive/Getty Images, p. 25 (bottom); © Topical Press Agency/Getty Images, p. 26; AP Photo, pp. 28 (top), 33; © Carl Mydans/Time & Life Pictures/Getty Images, p. 28 (bottom); © John Dominis/Time & Life Pictures/Getty Images, p. 30; © Keystone/Getty Images, p. 31; © Henny Ray Abrams/AFP/Getty Images, p. 32; © AFP/Getty Images, pp. 34, 64; © Steve Vidler/SuperStock, pp. 36–37; © Ben Yeh/AFP/Getty Images, p. 38; © Reinaldo Vargas/Art Directors, p. 39; © Chris Stowers/Panos Pictures, pp. 40, 43; © Kevin Morris/Stone/Getty Images, pp. 44–45; © Sam Yeh/AFP/Getty Images, pp. 47, 63; © Walter Bibikow/Taxi/ Getty Images, p. 51; © Yoshikazu Tsuno/AFP/ Getty Images, p. 52; © Yoshio Tomii/SuperStock, p. 53; © Stephen Shaver/AFP/Getty Images, p. 55; AP Photo/Annie Huang, p. 59; © Ximena Griscti/Alamy, p. 61; Audrius Tomonis—www.banknotes.com, p. 68.

Front cover: © Henry Westheim Photography/Alamy. Back cover: NASA.